# Lost

*Rocky I*

RESCUE STORIES

## Kyla Duffy and Lowrey Mumford

Published by Happy Tails Books™, LLC

Happy Tails Books™ uses the power of storytelling to effect positive change in the lives of animals in need. The joy, hope, and (occasional) chaos these stories describe will make you laugh and cry as you em*bark* on a journey with these authors, who are guardians and/or fosters of rescued animals. "Reading for Rescue" with Happy Tails Books™ not only brings further awareness to animal advocacy efforts and breed characteristics, but each sale also results in a financial contribution to rescue efforts.

**Lost Souls: Found!**™ Rocky Mountain Cocker Rescue RESCUE STORIES
by Kyla Duffy and Lowrey Mumford

Published by Happy Tails Books™, LLC. www.happytailsbooks.com

**Photo Credits:**

    **Front:**    Dexter

    **Back:**

        Left: Zenry
        Middle: Siggy
        Right: Blanche, Bess, and Beverly
        Top: Clover

    **Interior:**

        Title Page: Mariah and Tuxedo Jerry
        Dedication Page: Max and Roxy
        Story Introduction Page: Gus

**Publishers Cataloging In Publication Data Available Upon Request**

ISBN: 978-15023317-4-8

*Visit the following link for more information about the dogs, authors, and rescues featured in this book:*

http://www.happytailsbooks.com/about/authors/

# Dedication

Happy Tails Books™ appreciates all the contributors whose thought-provoking stories make this book come to life.

We would also like to thank Cindy Sweeney, Audra Bowen, Sherry Anisi, and Donna Brazill for volunteering their proofreading skills; and Kathryn Glass and the compassionate, hardworking volunteers at Rocky Mountain Cocker Rescue (RMCR) for their steadfast dedication to helping dogs in need. Battling America's homeless pet problem can sometimes feel overwhelming, but know that you are not alone, and you *are* making a difference, one life at a time.

You are our heroes.

# Table of Contents

# Introduction: His Rescue

In addition to being an introvert, as a child I was extremely shy. Animals were my best friends and often, by choice, my sole companions. Some of my first words were "King," "Penny," and "Blondie"—the names of the Cocker Spaniels in my life. Penny was my aunt's dog who died when I was only two years old. Some months later, Blondie arrived at the farm, and my aunt was amazed when the first word out of my mouth when I saw her was, "Penny!" She couldn't believe a toddler could remember such things.

One summer day when I was four, my constant companion, King, was strolling with me around the block (and probably raiding the neighbor's gardens of their peas and raspberries) when he was attacked by three or four bigger dogs. I vividly remember standing there, crying and screaming hysterically, while my little dog did his best to defend himself against the much larger dogs. Though they did not kill him, they chewed his back left leg to the bone. Despite his incredible pain, he let me love on him and try to help him as best as a four-year-old could while we waited for help to arrive.

The next day, my dad took King to the farm where he worked as a mechanic. I remember seeing King lying on a dog bed near my dad. Soon thereafter, my parents told me King had run away because they couldn't bear to tell me they had to put him down. We never had another family dog after that.

In 1993, my then-fiancé, Mike, and I inherited Sadie when her owners died within 14 months of each other. I had worked with one of her owners, who knew I loved Sadie very much, as she reminded me of the Cockers of my childhood, and I was grateful when we were asked to adopt her. Sadie gave us pure joy every day of her 11 years in our home. She died at age 15½ from perianal cancer.

Toward the end of the decade, I began volunteering at the Dumb Friends League to walk dogs a few evenings a week. It was a stepping stone for me to adopt another Cocker. One day, I found a dog named Molly shivering from fear in the back of her kennel. My heart melted, and she became my second dog. I was thrilled, but Sadie, who was used to being the only dog, merely tolerated Molly. Adopting Molly marked the end of my volunteering at the shelter because Mike, now my husband, was afraid I would continue to bring dogs home. He is no dummy!

Sadly, Molly was not a healthy dog, even at only two years old. She died three years later after we spent more than $7,000 trying to manage her inflammatory bowel disease. Her death was the first time in my life that my heart was truly broken.

In 2003, I adopted Spencer from a new Cocker rescuer in Aurora. Five years later, I was contacted by that same rescuer to help her out in a pinch. I ended up helping her for the remainder of the year, until I couldn't take the chaos anymore. I was ready to leave the rescue world behind me, when some people I had networked with during the year pleaded with me to start a new rescue. That is how Rocky Mountain Cocker Rescue (RMCR) was born in early 2009.

It was very important to me that RMCR be both legal and licensed. I applied for and was awarded a 501(c)(3) nonprofit charitable organization status, so donors could get a tax write-off.

We take our job as Colorado's only licensed Cocker Spaniel rescue seriously, which means we follow strict standards of care and documentation. Our mission and vision are based on Christian values. We rescue, foster, rehabilitate, and adopt out Cocker Spaniels into permanent, pre-qualified homes based upon our core values of integrity, reverence for all life, and respect for humans and animals, while providing excellence in all we do.

Rescue work is truly my passion in life. I was born to do it, no matter the inevitable heartache I sometimes experience when lives cannot be saved or rehabilitated. I am extremely blessed to work with an amazing group of people who step up to the challenges presented every single day. On those days when my heart is breaking, I read my favorite poem, "Footprints in the Sand," to remind myself that God Himself is carrying me through the tough times.

I have sincere, heartfelt thanks for everyone who contributed to this book and for the supporters of RMCR. If it wasn't for people willing to donate, volunteer, and foster dogs, we would not be able to save lives. Every one of you plays an important role in God's plan. Thank you from the bottom of my heart for answering the call to help.

We at RMCR hope these stories will inspire you to join us, if you haven't already. Please become part of our family by volunteering, fostering, and/or adopting. The life you save by your dog rescue activities may turn out to be your own.

 *Kathryn P. Glass, RMCR Founder and President*

# Rocky Mountain Cocker Rescue
## RESCUE STORIES

# First Sight

W hat Clover's experiences were before she came into rescue, I can only imagine, but from her condition, they couldn't have been good. Her owner, who bred her, kept dogs in crates in her garage and made money off the frequent birthing of puppies. There were many dogs who shared their lives and space with Clover in that cramped garage.

When the owner of the dogs died, her children didn't want them. They sold them all to other breeders, except for two, Clover and Chloe. Eight-year-old Clover was deaf and blind. Eleven-year-old Chloe was blind in one eye and partially deaf. Unwanted, they were sent to a shelter, which was probably better than the fate of the other dogs. The two girls soon won the hearts of the shelter workers, but they struggled to find forever families. Time passed, and the friends they had made wrote letters and emails to rescues all over the United States on their behalf. None of the rescues were willing to take on these two special-needs dogs.

One day, a small rescue in New Mexico agreed to take them because no one else would. Finally, someone wanted them! These girls were soon traveling with a truck driver volunteer from Indiana to Colorado, where they were scheduled to jump on their next transport to New Mexico. Bad weather set in on the mountain pass between Colorado and New Mexico, which turned out to be another stroke of luck. RMCR received a call for help and agreed to keep the two girls until the weather cleared, and they could continue their journey.

The pair stayed with a first-time RMCR foster mom, who fell in love with them, but when the mountain pass opened 12 days later, they continued their trip to New Mexico. After some much needed vet care, Chloe was adopted and now lives with Gail and her dog Wags, an older male Cocker Spaniel, but Clover remained unwanted. Meanwhile, in Colorado, the dog we were fostering got adopted. We love taking care of elderly and special-needs dogs. In our past, we had fostered six blind dogs, all of whom were successfully adopted, and when we heard about Clover, we were excited to take her in.

The foster mom who kept these girls during the bad weather just five months earlier, was now an RMCR director, and she immediately put plans in place to get Clover back to Colorado. A week later, Clover arrived on our doorstep. She was lying quietly in the back of a van in a wire kennel. The first thing I noticed were the cataracts in both her eyes. Beyond that, she was a beautiful red and very sweet. From the day she arrived, we knew this little girl was special. She was patient and accepting of anything that came her way. She quickly learned her way around the house and maneuvered outside well while doing her business. Her little stubby tail never stopped wagging. There was definitely a living, thinking force inside that quiet, unseeing head.

Every morning and evening, Clover and I went for a walk. These walks became the highlight of her day. As soon as the leash went on, she knew the fun was about to begin. She started learning about the world through her nose; it was like an explosion of her senses. She tracked rabbits and squirrels. She dragged me into people's yards and down the sidewalk, eagerly seeking the next new smell. She was exuberant! I only wished she could see the things she so loved to smell. She was missing the sight of trees and shrubs, where the bunnies and squirrels hid.

In our home, Clover received lots of love and touch. She had a funny way of expressing her desire to play. She would wave her head back and forth like Stevie Wonder and pound her rear foot against the floor. Sometimes she would put her head down on the floor and push herself around. She liked hugs, and I often made kissy sounds close to her ear. Clover was silent. She didn't bark or cry or whine. She took life at her own speed. She would explore the back yard and then slowly make her way back into the house. She wiggled away when arms held her, unsure of what was up and what was down.

RMCR decided she had so much life and joy in her that she deserved to be evaluated for cataract removal. She was deemed eligible, so the rescue started raising funds for the expensive surgery. Clover went to various pet fairs and met the many visitors to the RMCR booth. Her story and happy personality won many hearts, and donations began to swell. Seven weeks after her arrival to RMCR, she received her surgery.

I can hardly describe the feeling I had when she first looked at me. Her eyes were now brown, and they could see! At first, Clover followed her nose, cone to the ground, instead of looking up. She looked like she was plowing the ground with her protective collar, which quickly became a nuisance to her. She clunked her way around, knocking over things in her path. All of a sudden, she became more aware of her surroundings and quicker in her step. Since she could now *see* where she was going, she wanted to get there *fast.* She'd plow down the hall and catch our slow Chihuahuas in her "scooper"; they learned to stay out of her way. She became playful and started making little sounds.

When I would depart the house leaving Clover behind, she would make howling sounds at the door: "I want to go too! Take me! Take me!"

My heart leapt with each cry. Clover was becoming a real dog! At first, she tolerated her many eye drops patiently. After two weeks, she started turning and running away when she saw the bottles coming. She began protecting her chew bone with a soft growl, whereas before, the other dogs easily stole it from her. She began liking to be held. And then, she began giving me kisses. Incredible!

Nowadays, her tail wags at top speed, and she does a special little dance to get attention. It is wonderful to watch her grow and learn about the life around her. How boring it must have been in that cage in the garage, day after day, unable to see or hear. Clover is worth every penny the rescue spent to give her the gift of sight.

Gail, who adopted Chloe earlier in the year, lost Wags to cancer. At the same time, Chloe, now age 12, was quickly losing sight in her other eye. Gail wanted Chloe to have a companion, so she contacted RMCR asking if Clover or any other compatible Cocker was available. Not only did she learn Clover was available, but she also found out Clover could now see.

Eleven months after these girls were rescued and six months after they were separated, Clover and Chloe were brought back together, no longer as puppy mill crate-mates but as beloved companion animals. Now, these dogs have a life full of love and kindness to look forward to, both from the humans in their lives and from each other.

 *Linda Cline*

# Good as Gold

M y husband, Gery, and I retired and decided it was finally time to get the dog we had always wanted. We now had the time to spend with a dog, and we loved to camp, which we were sure our new pup would enjoy. We did not want to support puppy mills by buying a dog at a pet store; we knew a rescue was the way to go. Gery had loved his childhood Cocker Spaniel, who had grown up with him into adulthood, so choosing a breed was easy.

After a bit of Internet research, we decided to contact RMCR because they were designated as a 501(c)(3) nonprofit and seemed like a good place to start. When I emailed them and asked where their shelter was located, I was surprised to find that they had no shelter at all; each dog was fostered at a volunteer's home.

We went to two different adoption events that first Saturday and met many different Cocker Spaniels. How could we possibly choose? We loved them all but didn't have any strong preferences, so we decided to volunteer to get to know the dogs better. We figured that would lead us in the right direction.

At our first volunteer event, we met Kathryn, the president and rescue founder. As we helped show off four available foster dogs to passersby, Kathryn gave us a lot of interesting information about Cocker Spaniels and rescue. One dog went home with a pre-approved adopter that same day. Two of the remaining dogs were very active, and the third pretty much just watched everything from where he quietly sat. I pegged him as "Golden Boy" in my mind because the sun bounced beautifully off his pure gold body during the outdoor event.

When the event ended, Gery and I helped Kathryn load up all the gear, but she was short on room in her vehicle to take all three dogs. We offered to keep Chester, my Golden Boy, overnight and bring him to the next day's event. Along with some food and supplies, we brought Chester home, and everything went smoothly. He investigated the house and back yard, and he paid no attention to the cat, except for a bit of sniffing.

When we sat on the sofa to watch television, Chester jumped up and rolled himself into a loose ball between us. The whole experience was exactly what we were looking for, and I ended up calling Kathryn to let her know that Chester would not need to attend any further events. Although he was Golden Boy to me, Gery kept calling him Little Buddy, and that's what seemed to stick.

Buddy has now been with us for years and is the most beloved dog on the planet. Gery and I are still volunteering, but since moving to Florida, everything we do is by computer. I am now an RMCR board member and the human resources director. This means I set up adoption events and welcome new volunteers, encouraging them to pitch in and help in their own special ways. Additionally, I do a lot of administrative work remotely.

As Buddy aged, he was diagnosed with Cushing's disease, an adrenal condition that requires lifetime treatment. I know the disease will shorten his life a bit, but his medication keeps him acting like his old self, save for his needing to use the stairs to get onto the bed, whereas he used to jump onto it easily.

More recently, we adopted a little female Cocker Spaniel named Brandy, and she and Buddy have become devoted friends to each other. Buddy and Brandy fill our lives with joy and our home with love. Watching the dogs' body language and seeing their joy at camping, walking, riding in the car, and just being at home together with us makes our lives very happy.

 *Andrea Behr*

# Rough and Tumble

We have two daughters but no sons, so imagine our surprise when, at ages 55 and 58, my husband and I adopted a dog and found ourselves living with what seemed more like a teenage boy with really poor hygiene.

When we first met Cinnamon, we found him to be a sweet, delicate, little flower. An adorable blond with a white, freckled muzzle, his name seemed to suit him perfectly, but it only took about an hour for us to realize that perhaps he had been misnamed. His personality emerged—playful, goofy, and rough-and-tumble—which led us to re-name him Jake. This name was much more fitting of his personality.

Jake spent the first month with us holding on to our Havanese's tail while she dragged him up and down the stairs. During that same time, Jake had to have two "procedures" at the vet: one to remove a grass seed from his ear, which he brought home after his first hike, and another to remove a grass seed that had worked its way under the skin of his foot on his second hike. Since then, we've completed dozens of hikes with Jake, and he seems to be keeping all those vicious grass seeds at bay!

No matter how long or short our walks are, our white Havanese comes home in pristine condition, while Jake, on the other hand, returns with all four legs colored black all the way up to his shoulders. Only the top of his head and back remain blond. We don't know how this happens; somehow, filth just wicks up his legs. This bizarre phenomenon causes people to fall into fits of laughter when they see him out on trails.

We have never had such a filthy dog as Jake, but he couldn't be happier, and that's all that matters. In the past, he absolutely refused to get into water, and on one occasion, we had to have our 20-year-old daughter jump into a lake to retrieve the ball Jake refused to get. (She, by the way, retrieves really well!) But recently, at the Cherry Creek Reservoir Dog Park, he had a change of heart. He saw other dogs playing in the water and decided to take a flying leap, thinking they were in a shallow stream. Much to his surprise, the water was deep, and he had his very first swim, followed by several more leaps into the water to expand on his newfound skill.

Water cleanses most dogs, but not our Jake. Lucky for us, after every swim, he immediately finds dirt and rolls and rolls and rolls until he is chocolate brown, with sticks and leaves all over him, and is as happy as can be, hence, the teenage boy with poor hygiene.

For three years, Jake has filled our lives with love, play, laughter, and a whole lot of dirt and leaves. We are grateful for it all and for the special relationship we've developed with the carpet cleaning company!

 *Elisa Moran*

# Little Black Spot

I already had a sweet Cocker Spaniel named Maisy and two cats, Madison and Miss Kitty, but I thought adding one more canine would make my family complete. I started looking online, but every time I thought I had found "the one," he or she would get adopted before I even made an inquiry call. After three months of let-downs, I assumed the universe was telling me my family was already whole, but I decided to give my search one more week before putting it on hold indefinitely.

It was then that I saw him, a young Cocker available for adoption at Pueblo Welfare Animal Services (PAWS) in Pueblo, Colorado. In his photo, he looked like a little black spot in his cage. Because of his coloring, I couldn't make out any facial details. Nevertheless, I called PAWS and learned he was found as a stray, so they had no previous information about him. They assumed he was about three months old.

Although he was available for adoption, the shelter would only place a hold on him if I came to the shelter and requested it in person, which was a problem because the shelter was 2½ hours away. Knowing that this little boy was the one for me, I planned to take the next day off from work and make the trek to Pueblo. The next morning, I checked the PAWS website one last time before hopping in the car, and to my grave disappointment, the dog's photo was gone! I immediately telephoned PAWS and was told he was no longer there. I wasn't told were he went, nor did I ask because I assumed he had been adopted. I was devastated. I knew I was a good pet parent. Why did this keep happening to me?

Still within the final week I had allotted myself to look for a furry baby, I searched again online. Thank goodness I didn't give up because two days after the last blow to my heart, I saw the same picture of the little black spot in the cage. I could not believe it! Were my eyes deceiving me? Was it an old posting? No!

This time the dog was listed for adoption through RMCR. I emailed the rescue right away, noting that I had recently submitted an application regarding another Cocker who had been adopted. Shortly thereafter, I received a telephone call and found out RMCR took this sweet little boy because he was not adjusting well in the shelter. RMCR to the rescue! A volunteer drove to Pueblo, picked up the little black spot, and brought him to Parker, Colorado, to live with a foster family, who named him Benjamin.

Before I could meet my future fur-kid, I completed a rather enjoyable telephone interview with the RMCR adoption director. Then, we arranged the next step, a home visit in which Benjamin would meet my sweet girl, Maisy. I have to admit I was nervous, not about the home visit, but about how Maisy would react to Benjamin. After all, she was a princess and used to being an only dog.

When Kathryn of RMCR arrived at my townhome, we introduced Benjamin and Maisy out front. Within a few minutes, Maisy was okay with letting Benjamin into our home. While the two Cockers got to know each other, Kathryn and I had a delightful conversation. We both knew Benjamin was the missing piece of my family puzzle. A short time later, Kathryn left, but Benjamin stayed.

I quickly came to realize that this dog's personality was way too large to be a "Benjamin." He was more of a MacDaddy. Along with his big personality came many hurdles to cross. First, MacDaddy was a chewer, but after losing one expensive Oriental rug, three living room chairs, and countless shoes to his habit, we finally got that behavior under control.

More problematic than MacDaddy's chewing was his aggression, not toward the other animals in the house but toward me. Out of the blue, he would become aggressive, and I would usually end up getting bit. Several people, including my mother, suggested sending him back to the rescue, which surely would have taken him back, but how could I do that? He was my baby, and I refused to give up on him.

First, I tried a puppy obedience group, but due to MacDaddy's barking and what I perceived as his need to be the center of attention, we were relegated to a corner, away from the group, and given modified instructions. After four classes, it seemed the only thing we were gaining was more stress, so we dropped out.

Next, I hired an animal behaviorist, but she was just another disappointment. She was expensive and did not even physically work with MacDaddy, so I went to the Internet for help. I found a notice for a free seminar on living with an aggressive dog. The seminar was being held at a respected veterinary hospital, so I decided it was worth a try.

At the seminar, I was the only person in attendance, so I figured the instructor, Eric, would want to get me in and out as fast as possible. Fortunately, I was wrong. Eric spent 1½ hours with me discussing MacDaddy's behavior. Eric surmised that MacDaddy was likely experiencing fear-based aggression and provided some common sense methods to turn MacDaddy around. Needless to say, by the end of the seminar, I had appointed Eric as MacDaddy's new private trainer.

Eric came to the house that same week and worked on counteracting MacDaddy's aggression issues. He provided me with tools to neutralize MacDaddy's dominance and build his confidence. What a relief this training was! Finally, someone understood the problem and was able to help me implement solutions.

MacDaddy has been part of our clan for nearly five years now. We still have our difficult moments, and I think of him as my "spirited challenge," but I would not have it any other way. Despite all the struggles, MacDaddy's positives are tenfold! This mamma's boy loves to sleep on my lap, follow me from room to room, give me kisses, and snuggle close at bedtime. He is great with the cats, especially Miss Kitty, who is getting old and arthritic. MacDaddy plays very gently with her, rarely touching her other than licking her head, and she often returns his kisses.

Madison is much more outgoing. She and MacDaddy wrestle and chase each other. As for Maisy, I think overall she is glad she has a brother. Most days they play and sleep together, but there are days when she looks upon him with disdain, as any big sister might look at her little brother.

Back when it seemed every dog was unavailable to me, it wasn't that I didn't deserve another furry baby. The universe was simply making me wait for the little black spot to find his way home.

 *Pamela Maloney*

# Merry Little Dog

We have always had Cocker Spaniels. In 46 years of marriage, we have owned nine. Most were puppies we purchased from home breeders, until sadly, last year, our tri-colored Cocker, Scout, had to be euthanized after a long illness. Our black-and-white Cocker, Scamp, was lonely for his companion and seemed depressed. It was clearly time to find a new dog. Both of my adult children had rescued their dogs from humane societies, and I wanted to be a rescuer, too. I saw that RMCR had several nice dogs available, so on a cold January morning, I talked my husband into going to meet a few at a local Petco. This is where we met a black-and-white Cocker named Tank.

We adopted Tank and found him to be both a delight and challenge. According to RMCR, his family had surrendered him after keeping him outdoors for most of his life. His adoption write-up noted he liked to run. Was that ever an understatement! His first escape was on the first morning we had him. My husband tore a ligament in his knee chasing after him. Since then, he has escaped out the garage door several times, and he has escaped a couple times in the mountains.

Tank is an accomplished escape artist, and we must always be vigilant. We have extra leashes in our cars, in case of a break out. Fortunately, Tank will jump in the car if we catch up to him. None of my other dogs have tried to escape; they can be trusted off-leash. Not Tank! We always keep him on a leash and have installed several gates to thwart his ability to make a break for it.

Despite his tendency to run, Tank is a wonderful dog, and we are just beginning to discover his whole personality. Tank loves affection and wants snuggle-time every day. He loves to settle down on one of our laps to watch TV in the evening. He loves to be petted, hugged, and loved. He is also a very active dog. He loves walks in the park, visits to the mountains, and rides in the car. The adjectives that best describe Tank are raucous and rowdy. When it is time for a walk or dinner, he takes it upon himself to collude and conspire with Scamp to meet his objective.

Tank doesn't like to be out in any inclement weather, nor does he like to be confined in small areas or basements. He will go down in our basement if we are down there, but he clearly doesn't want to stay for any length of time. Tank has the complete run of our house and yard and takes full advantage of it.

He is a verbal dog, making many different sounds. He barks, whines, growls, and howls. He doesn't like our telephone answering machine and howls loudly when it announces an out-of-area call. He is very stubborn and doesn't like to move or be moved. At first, he objected vociferously if we attempted to move him, pick him up, or groom him. Fortunately, he now accepts our requests for him to move without growling. He even allows us to brush out his coat without complaint, and he loves going to be groomed every month.

Our dog loves to play ball with anyone and everyone who will throw him the ball. He has several balls he owns and protects. He carries them around in his mouth all day long. He also loves his stuffed toys and takes them all outside. We can frequently be found picking up abandoned toys in the yard.

My constant companion, Tank accompanies me everywhere. I once read that Cocker Spaniels are "…merry little dogs with ever-wagging tails." Tank is the poster dog for this statement! He keeps our other Cocker engaged with life. If we are out in public we can count on attracting a crowd of people asking to pet our dogs, who look so similar people think they are twins. Despite the initial challenges, we are totally in love with Tank and can't imagine life without him. After having many Cockers from breeders, we are so happy that we took a chance on rescue. There are so many dogs needing homes, and the rewards of providing that home for one are as numerous as are toys and balls in our yard.

 *Nancy Larson*

# Just Another Transport

The day I pick up Lucy starts out just like any other day. I arrive at a beautiful home in a lovely area of Denver, and a lady opens the door. She immediately starts crying; she is giving up her beautiful little Lucy, a black Cocker Spaniel. Despite my disdain for people abandoning their family members, I can't help but give her a hug and share some tears.

The woman has Lucy locked in the laundry room because, she tells me, Lucy is aggressive with strangers. She warns me, "Don't touch her, as she may bite," and advises me to sit down before she lets Lucy out.

I do as I'm told, but much to my surprise, Lucy runs right over to me and jumps up with a welcoming lick. "She is aggressive with our boy's friends. She is afraid of men, and we are afraid she will bite someone," the woman says.

*Oh my, we must have a very aggressive little dog here!* I think to myself.

After putting Lucy in the back of my car and starting my trek to her new foster mom's home, I am somehow drawn to this sweet little girl. She cries, and all I can think of is that she has no idea what is happening to her. She will not be sleeping in her little bed tonight; she will never see her family again—the family that's been hers for all of her six years. She will probably be in a cage tonight alongside the other dogs in her foster home. She'll surely feel alone and frightened.

After dropping her off and going home, I don't sleep the entire night thinking of that tiny black Cocker Spaniel, Lucy.

Within a day or two, I ask if I can foster Lucy. I'm cautious, as her former mom's words about her being aggressive bounce around in my head. After all, I don't really know this dog, and she could be mean. I carefully introduce her to my two granddaughters, ages seven and 10. She loves them both almost immediately. She also quickly adapts to my two 6'3" sons and befriends my other rescue dog, Wrigley. I don't see any of her supposed aggressive traits. She barks at new people, but that quickly transforms into friendly kisses.

After one month as my foster girl, there is no way I can possibly give her up, so Lucy becomes a permanent member of my family. Lucy loves to take walks, and for such a little Miss, she can run like the wind. She is very affectionate, always sitting close and giving kisses. When my granddaughters come to visit, she can hardly contain her joy. She sleeps with them or, should I say, on top of them. She loves her new family and her best friend, Wrigley.

I'll always wonder how this family could give Lucy up, or how any family can do so for that matter. Even so, I'm grateful that Lucy has been able to find a home with me.

 *Pat Guenther*

# Short Tails

**Pick Up The Pace:** My husband and I are fast-paced walkers. We do one-to-three miles, five-to-seven days a week. The first few times we walked with Harley, we both thought he might be the wrong dog for us. He poked along very slowly and stopped frequently. Out of frustration, we started bringing a baby stroller so when Harley, formerly known as Dipper, pooped out, we could continue walking while he had a rest in the stroller. Passersby would usually chuckle or smile knowingly, but Harley was totally unembarrassed about being "babied." This lasted about two weeks, after which Harley's endurance and speed improved so much that he could trot along with us the entire distance. Now, his butt wiggles when we pull out his leash; he loves his walks. We are glad we persevered through the embarrassing stroller rides because now we are one happy family! *-Laura and Neal Rathke*

**Unique Spaniel:** When our Cocker, Talley, passed away, we adopted Mercedes, a "Unique Spaniel" with short ears, a little snout, long legs, and a very long tail with a little pom-pom. The first night with us, Mercedes just sat in the middle of the room, until we moved her bed to her dad's side of the room, exactly where she wanted it. One day, we took Mercedes to the spa, where our other Cocker, Cinder, gets her regular groom, and she came out looking like the storybook character, Ramona Quimby—quizzical and comical. Mercedes is the new sentry at my office, keeping tabs on all the comings and goings. When she sees the delivery guys, who often give her treats, her tail wags so hard that it hits her sides. She loves walks and hikes and even goes running with me— pretty good for a nine-year-old dog. *-Lois & Dave*

# No Turning Back

The first time I met Wally, he stole my heart. Suzette, the RMCR foster coordinator, had come over to meet with me, my husband, and my three-year-old Cocker Spaniel, Casey, as we were considering becoming foster parents. I had asked Suzette to bring one of her foster dogs with her, so I could see how Casey would react. Guess who she brought? Yep, it was Wally. From the moment I saw him, I was smitten. He seemed so small compared to Casey. He loved to have his chin scratched and was so submissive when he approached that I had to wonder what type of life he led prior to being rescued. During our meeting, I more than hinted that Wally would be a great first foster for us, until Suzette finally exclaimed, "You can't have Wally!"

Suzette had pulled Wally from the Longmont Humane Society, despite how sick he had been, and had taken him in for the rescue. After 7½ years of neglect, Wally was a mess. He didn't even look like a Cocker. His eyes, ears, and kidneys were infected, and his testicles were attached to internal organs. The rescue paid for an operation to neuter him, remove some intestine, and take out a squeaky toy he had previously swallowed. He also had six teeth removed. Suzette had been fostering him and nursing him back to health.

After Suzette left with Wally, I thought about him all the time. In addition to his recent surgery, Wally's left eye and jowl drooped for some unknown reason, and he had a very bad skin infection. My heart went out to him; he just couldn't catch a break.

On the RMCR Facebook page, I learned that Wally was going to be at an adoption event in Highlands Ranch, so I decided I should pay him a visit. At the event, I felt a sense of loss when I saw a family interact with Wally, as I feared they might adopt him, and he would no longer be available to me.

I had yet to admit publicly that I was so smitten with Wally, but in speaking with Suzette at the event, I saw my chance to spend more time with him. It turned out that Suzette was going on vacation and looking for someone to watch Wally while she was away. Of course, I was all for it; I was ecstatic when she contacted me later that week to confirm.

When Suzette dropped off Wally for the week, she told me he had a family who was going to adopt him once she returned. I asked Suzette where Wally should sleep, and she said in his crate, as that is where the potential adopters would have him sleep. Upon hearing that, I was resolute not to let him go home to this new family. Wally had been left outside in a kennel for years. He had not been loved and cared for as he should have been. Now that he was rescued, Wally deserved to sleep wherever he wanted, and he should get the attention he now craved.

Wally was supposed to be with us for seven days, but after the first day, I knew we were in big trouble. The thought of having to say goodbye to Wally broke my heart, and by the end of the week, I knew he should stay with us. Who could take better care of him than us? Fortunately, Suzette saw the writing on the wall. It also didn't hurt that the family interested in Wally backed out after learning he was occasionally marking indoors.

After being part of our family for almost a year now, Wally is doing great. He started having seizures shortly after we adopted him, but a neurologist helped us get his illness under control. He gets drops for dry eye twice a day, thyroid medication, and immunotherapy. He gained some much needed weight—maybe a little too much—but he looks good to me. He finally beat (we hope) the skin infection we helped him battle for many months, and he touches the hearts of most everyone he meets.

Wally and Casey have grown on each other, and although it took Casey some time to adjust to the idea of having Wally as a sibling, they are now pretty good buddies. Wally started attending doggie daycare with Casey a couple days a week and seems to really enjoy it. He is not thrilled with naptime, however, which requires him to be in a crate, so we break him loose during that time and bring him back when his friends are ready for afternoon play in the romper room.

Wally is obviously enjoying his life, which makes me very happy. He has his own special bed he loves, and we have put an ottoman at the foot of our bed, so he can join Casey and us whenever he wants. He loves chasing his doggie brother around the house and thinks nothing of dripping large amounts of water wherever he goes after he drinks. Of course, the paralysis on his left side doesn't make drinking easy, so we have a handy little mop that is always at the ready. Problem solved! Wally has modified the game of fetch. While he did learn to chase the ball, he has little interest in bringing it back. Instead, he takes it to a corner of the yard and chews on it to his heart's content.

I have to admit that, prior to having Wally, I didn't want to adopt an older dog. Colby, my previous Cocker, was with me for 16½ years, and I didn't want to have to deal with the aging process and the loss again for a very long time. Nevertheless, when Wally came into my life, my heart took over and there was no turning back.

 *Kathleen Kellams*

# A Big Heart

Rusty was a parti-colored, rambunctious Spaniel when I adopted him five years ago. A good sprinter, he loved the open spaces and the hiking trail near my home, no matter if we were out in daylight or in the cool darkness at the end of a day. He was always ready for a walk. Rusty was best buds with my two cats, often sleeping side-by-side with them, but his favorite spot was beside me.

When I opened the front door, Rusty often darted out to check for fallen goodies at the nearby dumpster. With the door still open, I would tell people, "He'll be back," and within a few moments, he'd come scurrying back to be by my side. When I was in the kitchen, Rusty was always hovering. He absolutely loved watermelon, devouring it until he hit the green rind and then coming away with a big, red smile.

One summer, there was so much smoke and ash from fires in our part of Colorado that nobody was outside of its reach. Rusty developed a slight cough that autumn, for which I scheduled a vet visit. X-rays revealed an oversized heart—likely congenital—and mild fluid buildup in his lungs. The veterinarian prescribed medication and a limited lifestyle.

As the smoke cleared, life returned to near-normal. Having a big heart is usually a good trait, but not for our four-legged friends when it's in a literal sense. For almost two years after his diagnosis, Rusty lived the best life he could, until his big heart could function no more.

While not as long as I would've liked, I am grateful for the time I had with Rusty. Some may call pets like Rusty "pets with problems," but I call them "pets with benefits," as their challenges allow them to give us so much more on so many levels. They allow us to learn and to love in ways we never knew we could. I think they know that, too.

 *Char H.*

# Snow Survivor

I was looking for a dog like my previous Cocker, Buster, so I reached out to RMCR to see if they had a male, buff Cocker with a long tail. I was told that they currently did not and that finding a male, buff Cocker with a long tail could take years. When the RMCR volunteer I spoke with asked if I would consider another dog, I said, "Sure."

I was open to other dogs, but none of the dogs in the pictures the rescue sent me felt like the dog I was supposed to have. Three weeks later, I received a call from RMCR telling me they had a nine-month-old, female, buff Cocker with a long tail coming in from Utah. There was only one catch: she was not a purebred Cocker. She also had some King Charles Cavalier in her. The shelter she came from called her Callie.

We arranged to meet Callie at Petco in Highlands Ranch, Colorado, and I arrived early with anticipation. Callie was skittish and shy, but she appeared to have bonded with her foster mom, who mentioned that Callie was a little ornery. Callie had chewed some of her foster mom's books, socks, and shoes, and the cables to her computer, but I didn't care. I adopted her immediately.

Callie acclimated easily, except that she remained skittish around new people, especially men. It took Callie more than a week to allow my husband to get close to her. She wouldn't let him take her out to potty or for a walk, but she was surprisingly easy for me to potty-train.

Callie joined our family in February, and we found her habit of eating snow and then scrounging around in it for leaves, twigs, and bugs to be telling of her former life. It struck me that she probably had to do that to survive, and the behavior inspired me to want to learn more about her past. RMCR had no information about her outside of the paperwork they had received when they picked her up in Utah, which they then provided to me. This paperwork included a vaccination sheet from a vet in Vernal, Utah, so I called them to inquire. The good news was that they remembered Callie because she was so cute but also so skittish and timid. The bad news was that they also didn't know how she had ended up in rescue. What they did know was the name of the small, home-based rescue that had originally brought her into their office for vaccinations.

I did some sleuthing and found the phone number to the small rescue in Vernal called Darlene & Tim's Pet Samaritan. After leaving a few messages, Darlene called me back and recounted what she knew about Callie. Apparently, Callie had landed in a high-kill shelter in Provo, Utah, after wandering around as a stray in the dead of winter. That shelter had Callie's owner's information but failed to reach them after several attempts. Although Callie was underweight and extremely skittish upon intake, the shelter attempted to adopt her out. She sat in the shelter huddled in the back of her kennel for more than a month, but no one wanted to adopt such a frightened, anti-social-looking dog.

It seemed Callie's time on this earth was nearing its end, as the shelter couldn't hang on to her forever, but by some stroke of luck, Darlene found out about Callie and took her in. Darlene & Tim's Pet Samaritan then attempted to adopt Callie out from their small shelter, but again, she sat in a kennel for more than a month. Darlene and Tim were surprised that no one was interested in adopting Callie because the young dogs usually got adopted quickly. Plus, Callie was so darn cute. They surmised that because Callie was so timid, folks just thought she would have too many issues.

Darlene and Tim didn't know what to do with Callie, so they reached out to RMCR. Darlene told me she didn't think that RMCR would rescue her because she was not a full-blooded Cocker, but to her surprise, they welcomed her with open arms and said they thought they had someone who would adopt her right away. That someone was me!

Callie has brought so much happiness and joy to our lives, and I was so impressed with our RMCR experience that

I became a volunteer. I'm thankful I wasn't discouraged by Callie's shyness because she has turned out to be the best dog. She loves to play and loves her walks. Snow, sleet, rain, or hail can't keep her from them; she just loves the outdoors. She is still somewhat timid but warms up to new people more quickly now.

I take Callie everywhere I can. The only drawback is that anyone who sits in my passenger seat has to share it with Callie. We're working on moving her into the back, but making our passengers share a seat is a small price to pay for such a great dog.

There is no doubt in my mind that God intended Callie to be with us. After being rejected by her owners, she outsmarted the elements in Utah while on the loose and survived two shelters. How odd is it that as young and as cute as she was (and still is), *no one* would adopt her from two shelters? God was clearly saving her for us.

 *Liz Koury Pestinger*

# Washcloth Wiggins

I have adopted many different breeds of dogs throughout my life, so when my husband wanted a Cocker Spaniel, I went right to the Internet and found RMCR. After a thorough interview process including phone calls and a home check, we finally adopted Koby, a beautiful, loving, white dog with red spots.

Koby was extremely healthy until two years ago, when the veterinarian found glaucoma in his right eye. It was beyond repair and had to be removed. He later developed glaucoma in his left eye, which we were able to save, even though it has gone blind. Despite his lack of sight, his behavior hasn't changed one bit, and I sometimes forget he's blind. He still follows me everywhere. I read a lot of books on how to deal with a blind dog and found it is not hard. The only changes I've had to make are that I talk more; I count the stairs for Koby and tell him where I am and what we are doing.

Koby, who is now 13½, loves to play with his new brother, Mr. Wiggins, a six-year-old Cavalier King Charles Spaniel. Koby gives Mr. Wiggins daily licking baths, and now Mr. Wiggins washes Koby's face, too. They like to be next to each other and are perfect friends. When I tell Mr. Wiggins to go get Koby from upstairs, he runs up and licks Koby's face to wake him up, and then they come down together. They love walking together and occasionally eat from one another's dish, as if making sure they have the same food.

When I had surgery, Koby was right by my side. He gave me extra kisses to let me know he was there for me, and he did the same for my husband after his surgery and many hospitalizations. To me, Koby and Mr. Wiggins are like little, furry people instead of animals. They talk through their eyes and their actions, and in this way, they show their unconditional love.

When my grown children visited from out of state, I was a little nervous because my grandson, Alex, was only a year old, and I didn't know how Koby would react to him. To my delight, Koby let Alex do anything to him. He didn't even mind when Alex played with his toys. His behavior with Alex reinforced my belief in this wonderful, loving breed. Cockers are kind, loving, faithful, energetic, and sympathetic—great dogs all around.

I have come to find that Cocker Spaniels and Cavalier King Charles Spaniels are the breeds for me. When it is time for Koby to go to the Bridge and get his wings, I will go back to RMCR to adopt another. Koby is my angel and Mr. Wiggins is following his example. I am one very happy mom of both my Spaniels.

 *Gloria Kotecki-Slomski*

**Author's Note:** *After writing this story, I had to put my sweet, little Koby down. It broke my heart, but he was in pain and had trouble breathing. I know he no longer blind, running free and happy. As for me, I'll adopt another RMCR Cocker soon.*

# Guidance from Above

Athena needed a dog sitter while her foster mom went out of town. Her owner had surrendered her to the rescue with matted, overgrown fur, but she was otherwise healthy and happy. She had arrived with good manners and several tricks up her paw and was known to be a quick learner who was eager to please. It would have been a no-brainer for us to step up and help, but the request went out just two months after our beautiful Cocker, Meikia, had gone to the Bridge, and my husband, Dean, and I were still grieving.

Meikia had come to us 1½ years prior as a foster dog. At the time, she had been fighting for her life because of illness and infections. Throughout all her treatments, she never once complained or cried out, and she became immediately attached to Dean. She would "talk" to him when he got home and then take up a position on his lap, with her paws on his chest and her eyes locked on his, as though she just couldn't get enough of him. It hadn't taken long for us to adopt her.

Shortly after adopting Meikia, we found she had heart issues, and we went the distance and more to help her have as long and healthy a life as possible. She was a strong and brave girl, and she never fought the help we gave her. Despite our efforts, she went to the Bridge after being with us a short 1½ years and at only eight years old, and we were devastated.

Even so, upon hearing about Athena, I felt something urging me to broach the dog-sitting matter with Dean. I think I was hoping Athena could help heal his broken heart. When I mentioned Athena's situation, Dean said he wasn't sure if he wanted to see her, let alone bring her into the house for any length of time. But, in the end, we agreed to take her and treat her with all the love she deserved while her foster mom was away.

We quickly came to find that Athena is nothing like Meikia, which is how she initially crept into our hearts in just three days. Being only two years old, she still had the energy, sass, and playfulness of a puppy. She was on the go all day long playing with our other two Cockers.

Needless to say, we quickly went from being dog sitters to being parents. Since then, we've seen many moments when we have felt that Athena is getting some direction or hints from our angel above. For example, she has taken Meikia's pose on Dean's lap several times, staring at him just as Meikia had. Also, the first time Athena rode with us in the car, she went right to the cup we had kept for Meikia to drink from and looked at Dean until he put some of his water into it. She drank from the cup instead of from the bowl we had provided for her. And the only blanket she likes to cuddle under is Meikia's special one.

Coincidence? We think not. God works in mysterious ways, and so does our girl, Meikia.

This sweet, happy girl has adjusted well to our home. She lets our alpha male, Bailey, know she is the new boss, and he lets her get away with it. Our other female, Bella Luna, plays with Athena endlessly when Athena isn't busy hoarding her toys. She loves everyone—from children to dogs—and she is great off-leash, roaming close by our sides. The only thing that bothers her is loud noises like lightning, thunder, and fireworks. This is new for us, as we've never had a dog who is bothered by the racket, but we've found that all we need to do is keep her close and cuddle with her until the noises stop.

We are smitten with this 14-pound bundle of Cocker and plan a long and loving life with her. We expect to have many fun adventures in the years to come.

 *Dean and Linda Parker*

# The Payoff

In our search for a companion for our black-and-tan Cocker Spaniel, Winnee, we decided to try a rescue dog. We found RMCR and innocently inquired about a black Cocker-mix, who had been brought in from another state. Chico, now our Rocky, was described as a friend to all. He had been found underweight and running free.

The dog sounded simple enough, and, of course, he would be no trouble, as we knew *all about* dogs. If we just fed him, loved him, and walked him, all would be well, right?

Upon meeting Rocky in the parking lot of our veterinarian's office, we immediately noticed that the "mix" part of him might be standard Poodle. "Great!" we agreed. "High intelligence will just make things easier."

After the rescue volunteers drove away and left us with our new dog, we turned to walk Rocky into the veterinary office for shots and a checkup. Coming toward us was a Boxer-looking dog with his owners. The dog returned Rocky's friendly bark with an attack, and the checkup turned into a bite repair. From that day forward, Rocky's fear has turned him into the aggressor, which has made for some interesting walks. He barks. Then Winnee barks back at him. Their leads tangle, and we turn in circles to unwind them as we apologize to passing neighbors. Nose to nose, the dogs greet Rocky and Winnee, and Rocky realizes it's okay. That is, until the next morning when the spectacle begins anew.

We can't help but wonder what happened in Rocky's past to send him into a frenzy each time he hears a coffee pot steaming, a plane flying overhead, or birds chirping outside. Had he never heard these things before? Little by little, he has accepted each new sound with an "It's okay, Rocky," and a calming pat. We've yet to find words to reassure Rocky about sprinkler systems. Rocky is determined to kill the spray and protect his territory. A nearby golf course for Rocky is a never-ending supply of sprinkler "enemies" to bark at and battle.

Rocky is curious and cautious about everything. With his keen intelligence, great eyesight, and detective nose, he can find any toy we hide or ball we throw. On the downside, like a two-year-old, he will also gladly unpack my purse, suitcase, or the groceries I am carrying.

Rocky growls when we try to take items back from him, and at first, that made us afraid. After noticing his tail wagging at top speed along with the growl, we realized that he enjoys the game, and that's just how he plays. Every evening, the "wait" games are on. We hide and throw balls for both dogs, and they compete to see who returns them for a treat first. Rocky's last chore of the evening is to bring the squeaky ball and settle in at the foot of the bed.

Rocky is now more than a companion to our other Cocker, Winnee. As she has aged, we have discovered she has genetic retinal degeneration, which no surgery can repair. Rocky's alertness and barks keep Winnee in the know and help her to walk, play in the yard, and keep us entertained.

As for Rocky, his eyes tell his true story. While all Cockers melt you with their searching eyes, Rocky's seem to say, "Do you still love me?" And with a pat, a hug, or a treat, we try to say, "Of course, we do."

Somewhere a person did not recognize the depth of this dog's love, and his desire for a human companion, which turned out to be a stroke of luck for us. When Rocky snuggles up to us at TV time, his head goes on our laps, and he lets out a deep, contented sigh. His eyes roll back, and he sleeps soundly. I believe he knows he is safe and loved by us, and we feel the same way about him. Like we were told it would, patience and time have paid off.

 *Lisa Myles*

# I Like Mike

R eally, I love my Mike. Before he came to our home, I had a few dogs in my life. I had a small female Cocker named Lady, but after losing her to a heart problem, I moved on to a different breed—a Golden Retriever. She'd been over-bred and needed a happy retirement, which we gladly provided.

After our Golden went to the Rainbow Bridge, I wanted another Golden, but my husband, Fred, wanted another Cocker. Ultimately, I saved Casey, a 10-month-old Golden, from certain death, and we got a Border Collie/Australian

Shepherd-mix aptly named Buddy, to be Casey's companion. Tragically, we lost Buddy when he was only 20 months old.

After Buddy passed, I went on a mission to get my Casey a new companion. This is when Mike entered our lives. I typed "Cocker Spaniel rescue" into a search engine, and RMCR showed up. I contacted the rescue, and we determined it would be a good idea for me to foster some dogs until I found one who fit into our home perfectly. I didn't have a special dog picked out from those listed on the website, and I was in a good position to become a volunteer. Shortly thereafter, a wonderful woman from RMCR brought over a little white dog with spots to be my first foster. My Golden, Casey, followed that little mess right into the back yard. He had been so sad before, but now he was happy again. I told the lady, "Don't even put him on the RMCR site. He is not leaving here."

Since the dog was rescued and brought right to my home, we got to name him, but I drew a blank. Nothing seemed right, until my daughter-in-law said, "Mike." It fit him perfectly, so he became Mike.

This little soul had been lost, but someone found him as a stray right here in Colorado. RMCR drove to the animal shelter, picked him up, and brought him right to my home. I took him to the veterinarian for his exam, and we determined that he needed some serious help. His teeth needed cleaning, and both ears needed to be flushed because they had bacterial infections.

We went home, and while we waited for his appointment for both procedures, I bought some dental sticks for Mike. I was going to ask the veterinarian about giving them to my little buddy, but sneaky Mike saw the bag hanging off the counter and decided not to wait for the veterinarian's approval; he ate them all!

When I took him to the veterinarian, his teeth were spotless, and the cleaning no longer necessary. His ears were a different story. They were hard to clear up, but, finally, they improved. Once he had a clean bill of health, we were able to make his adoption official.

Mike is great with people, including our two young grandsons, and he is good with all the RMCR foster dogs who have entered our home since we adopted him. There have been other RMCR dogs who have touched our hearts, but none like my Mike. I do like Mike. Really, we all do.

 *Donna Kunkel*

# Short Tails

**Just Couldn't Wait:** After losing our two beloved Cockers within four months of each other, we were set on waiting a while before getting a new fur-baby. That lasted about five days. When I saw Doodle on the RMCR website, I instantly fell in love. My husband, Dave, told me not to get attached, in case she didn't work out, but when we met her at a Petco adoption event, she put her paws on Dave's leg and licked his face, sealing the deal. Her name is now Ellie, and she is a wonderful, frustrating, ornery part of our family. She has destroyed just about everything, but that's just part of her charm. Seven months after adopting her, we adopted another Cocker named Gracie, and between our two girls, we can say that rescuing dogs has been one of the most rewarding experiences of our lives. -*Deanna Tice*

**The Journey Begins:** Poor A.J. had been returned again and was getting a pretty bad rap for snapping at a child. He was small, oddly-colored, and rambunctious. Not at all what I had in mind when I set out to adopt a dog similar to my recently departed friend. After a rescue volunteer had suggested him to me, I kept looking but finally agreed to meet him. He turned out to be loving and gentle, and his pleading eyes captured my heart. His name is Buddy now, and he is all that and more. He has great energy that keeps me moving each day. My constant companion is loved by everyone he greets. Buddy has his new forever home, and our wonderful journey has begun! -*Cynthia McGann*

# Cat and Cocker

W hen I arrived at Critter Fest to represent our local animal shelter, I had no idea that I would find a new love. Next to our booth was RMCR, one of my other animal rescue favorites; in fact, I had brought a donation check with me for them. My friend, who was also volunteering at the event, spotted my new love first: "Isn't she adorable?"

Yes, she was, and beautiful, too. Her foster mom told me she had been found as a stray on the other side of the state. She was matted and smelly, but the rescue had cleaned her up and shaved her free of matts. Her foster mom said she was a gentle, sweet snuggler who likes to share not only your bed, but also your pillow. I was hooked as I held her and walked her, and soon, I texted my husband, Greg, about this little girl.

"So, we're getting another dog?" he asked. "Do you think she'll fit in with our Lhasa, Joey, our other rescued Cocker, Lily, and Walter, our huge old cat?"

We talked about the pros and cons of adopting another dog over breakfast on Sunday morning. We were most concerned about how Walter would feel about her. Our other dogs are social butterflies, so that was not a concern, but Walter...How would he accept another dog? And did this cutie know anything about cats? We decided that adopting her would probably not work out, so we rescinded our offer to adopt her that same morning.

Walter was our priority, but the thought of not adopting this dog upset me so much that I was speechless on the ride home, a rare occasion. Finally, I told Greg I knew this dog needed us, and I thought giving up was a mistake. I was sick to my stomach and in my heart at the thought of it. All our adopted pets had adjusted to each other just fine; why would this dog be any different?

Greg asked, "Do you want to go back?"

I said, "We have to."

Greg turned the car around, and I frantically tried to reach the rescue to let them know we were coming back. I couldn't reach anyone, and I worried our new dog had already stolen someone else's heart, so when Greg dropped me in the parking lot, I ran to the booth to declare my love for this beautiful dog. To my relief, she was still there.

Our new little Abbey girl, spelled in honor of the famous Beatles album, still needed to get a clean bill of health from the veterinarian, so we waited patiently for her to become officially adoptable. In the meantime, we purchased all things dog. She needed just the right collar, bed, blanket, bowl, and new toys free of other dog slobbers. We wanted her new forever home to feel perfect from the start.

Abbey has now been with us for nearly a month, and we're still blending her into our lives. She and Walter are a non-issue these days. She sniffs Walter wherever he is sprawled out, and Walter takes a half-hearted swing at her, but her growling and snarling and his hissing and spitting are all gone. She sleeps in Walter's bed from time to time all curled up in a ball. Personally, I think it is hilarious, though I'm not sure how Walter feels about it.

We are still finding Abbey's quirks. For example, she doesn't like Chihuahuas, which is unfortunate because there are many Chihuahuas at the dog park. We'll never know her background, but we are working with her as issues come up. The next hurdle is determining who's the alpha in our pack, now that Abbey is comfortable enough to get bossy.

Abbey has a mellow, graceful aura about her, and everyone who meets her falls in love. As I write this, she is stretched out under my feet, snoozing next to our other Cocker, who is happy to have a friend to help chase bunnies in the yard.

 *Donna Brazill*

# Two Perspectives: Carmie

### The Adopters: Carmie's Karma

Life's road takes some surprising turns. Ours took an abrupt detour last August after a happy celebration weekend with family and friends.

We had two wonderful rescued Cockers: Missy was 16, and Lilo was 12. Missy had been living life to the fullest, enjoying her backyard fish pond and going on RV trips. Anyone who has had a fish pond knows how much time and care it requires. We were willing to do this for Missy because it helped her remain active. Missy loved going outside with us daily when we fed the fish and checked up on them.

Upon returning home from our visit with friends and family, we noticed that one of the two pond pumps was not working. We did not take time to fix it because over that weekend, Missy fell ill. Our trip to the pond that Wednesday turned out to be Missy's last. We sat next to the pond and held her as we said goodbye.

The following morning, we went out to visit the fish without our faithful assistant, and the second pump had also broken, as if life was sending us a message. With Missy gone, we no longer needed to maintain the labor-intensive pond, so we removed it and put in a simple water feature in Missy's honor.

That winter seemed to be harsher than usual, so we planned an RV trip to warmer weather. We took Lilo for a quick check at the veterinarian's office because she had started exhibiting some unusual mouth tremors. The veterinarian cleaned her teeth and removed a small gum growth. The lab results were inconclusive, so the veterinarian told us to not to worry, to take the trip and enjoy the warmer weather.

During the 10-week trip, Lilo took daily walks and lay outside in the sun, but within days of returning home, she started acting differently. We went to the veterinarian's office again, but this time, the visit lasted for four hours and resulted in a lot of crying. The growth in Lilo's mouth had most likely been cancerous after all and had metastasized to her liver. She was too anemic and weak to recover.

We were lucky to have several more days with Lilo, doing her favorite things: taking her on car rides and letting her snuggle between our legs. She left us on April 26th, which turned out to be an important date for several reasons.

Although we had agreed not to get another dog, my partner, Pody, had quickly begun secretly checking the RMCR website daily, where she found one female named Carmella, who repeatedly stood out. We inquired about her, and her foster mom, Donna, told us Carmella was a loving "Velcro dog" who had several ongoing medical issues.

We knew we wouldn't mind her clinginess, but we wondered whether we could deal with more veterinary visits after what we had recently gone through. We decided to take a gamble and drove four hours to visit Donna and Carmella. Carmella was extremely attached to Donna, so it was hard to assess her temperament. Donna tried to put some space between her and Carmella, and we noted that Carmella was very shy. She preferred hanging out with her foster brothers rather than coming to us, but we got in a few pets.

We were unsure about adopting a dog who paid such little attention to us, but when Donna shared Carmella's arrival date, we were sure it was a sign. What was the chance of our meeting a dog who had come into the rescue on the same day our Lilo had passed?

When it was time to go, Carmella followed us to the front door. Donna said she hadn't done that with anyone before. Was that another good sign? Perhaps.

We told Donna we would think it over and give her a call. She told us she was up at 4:30 a.m. every morning, so at 6:00

a.m. the next morning, we were on the phone with Donna telling her, "Yes!"

We wanted Carmella, now "Carmie," to be ours.

*Laurel Haack and Pody Woodman*

## The Adoptee: A New Life

These two new people came into my life like a whirlwind. I really did not like the long ride back to my forever home, so I made one of them sit in the back seat with me to reassure me the entire time. I was exhausted when we arrived home.

They let me sleep on their bed the first night, but I peed on it because I forgot to wake up. They were okay about that, but they put these plastic pads on it the next day. That must be something people do because it made no sense to me.

Since arriving at my forever home, I have learned it is okay to travel more than 50 feet from either of my new parents, and I sometimes forget I am in the yard all by myself. I like my new name, Carmie, but if I am exploring and someone calls it, I am sometimes so preoccupied that I don't hear it. That's when my people start calling me Carmella Jane. When I hear that—and I always do—I come running immediately!

I have lucked out this summer because it seems like we are always going on vacation. My people have a big RV, and I get to go in it all the time. I know when a big trip is coming because my people start carrying lots of things into the RV. I just make sure they remember my food because eating is my favorite thing to do. I found out that they won't get up and feed me at 4:30 a.m. like Donna did, but I guess I can live with that.

My people also took me to a ranch, where I was able to become part of a pack with the dogs who lived there. Every morning I got up and joined them for the day's ranching events. I quickly learned not to walk or roll in cow pies because otherwise I would have to get a bath.

My people also took me to a lake and blew up a big blue thing. Then they put this contraption, a life vest, on me and told me it was okay. They walked away from me into the water and called for me to come; they didn't know that I do not like walking in water. I'm more of a Cocker than a Spaniel, if you know what I mean. They finally picked me up and put me in the blue thing, and you know what? After a while, I really started liking it.

I found out that all I have to do is be good, obey when I am told to do something, and give lots of love in order to get to do all these new, exciting things with my people. They're a whirlwind, for sure, but I love it!

 *Carmie*

# The Gardener

Emmylou's story started several years ago, when for unforeseen reasons, she ended up in a small, dirty, run-down shelter outside of Cheyenne, Wyoming.

A volunteer from Black Dog Animal Rescue made a trip over to see the shelter and found several dogs in filthy living conditions. She took it upon herself to safely remove all the dogs from the shelter and tried placing them in local foster homes. She called several breed-specific rescues for help and found RMCR, which brought Emmylou to one of their Denver foster families.

We had just lost our beloved Golden Retriever, and we both wanted to "downsize." My husband had Cocker Spaniels growing up, and I had always admired their cuteness. We applied for a little girl through RMCR and got added to the queue, but we didn't have much hope of adopting her because there was already a waiting list.

Then, we got a call about this cinnamon-colored little girl who was coming down from Wyoming, and our hearts danced with joy!

We picked up Emmylou about a week after she arrived in Denver, and she made herself at home right away, jumping up into the bay window and surveying her new neighborhood. She was well-mannered and loving right from the start. She couldn't get enough of wandering around the back yard, as if she had never seen such a delightful place to play.

Emmylou loves vegetables, so I call her my little Cocker-bunny. She camps out in front of the refrigerator waiting for someone to open it and give her a cold, wet carrot stick from the ones we keep at eye-level in a bowl for her.

Emmylou loves green beans, too, so I thought planting green beans in our garden would be a great idea. I realized my plan wasn't flawless when, after watching me carefully pick just the right size green beans for Emmylou's supper, she decided to help herself to them, too. She started out just sampling them by munching them on the vine, but then she realized that she could pull the entire vine out of the ground and carry it to a cool place in the yard, where she could savor several green beans at a time. Needless to say, I wasn't too happy with my new "helper." A makeshift fence kept her from pulling out the vines, but she could still jump it and sample her favorite veggies. I knew then that planting carrots would only produce a little digger who wanted to get her own carrots out of the ground, so that idea went to the composter!

Emmylou now wanders through the gigantic tomato plants that tower several feet above her, and I am hoping that she doesn't take a liking to the little, red, cherry tomatoes that hang down low enough to tempt her. She did try a green one once, but the disgusted look on her face said I didn't have to worry about her eating more of the sour little morsels.

We all love summer with the fresh fruit and veggies it brings. Our little gardener especially likes the cantaloupe and watermelon her daddy feeds her off his fork. It is so cute that I can't scold them! They have this game where Emmylou sits quietly waiting for a small bit of fruit. After her dad gives it to her, she sneaks over to the other side of him and looks up like he's supposed to believe she is a different dog who just looks like Emmylou. We have named the "other" dog "ET" (Emmylou's Twin). They both get little bites, and we get a laugh at her cleverness!

 *Carolyn Pittman*

# Those Soft, Brown Eyes

One night almost three years ago, my buff-colored angel trotted through the front door and into my life. For me, it was a miracle and an answer to my prayers. I had contacted RCMR and asked if they could help me find a male Cocker Spaniel in need of a home, preferably a buff one. I know it shouldn't matter how he looked, but I wished to come as close as possible to Murphy, my beloved companion from 12 years past.

Of course, each dog has his or her own special identity, which can never be fully duplicated, but I had a dream. And then, there he was! Stunning in beauty and in his resemblance to Murphy, this gorgeous, fluffy figurine pranced into my arms to stay.

My priority was to create the ultimate win-win situation by saving a beautiful animal and saving myself in the process, and that is truly what was to become of my life with Chester. Whether he's sneaking me the occasional glance of approval while wolfing down his dinner or giving me nice, thoughtful, loving kisses while fixing those big, brown eyes on me— there are too many instances of the joy he brings to mention, and I am certain many more are to come.

My Chester has been the greatest gift I've ever received. If there is one word to sum up what we mean to each other, it is *love*. Our love is not only irreplaceable, but it is something I appreciate now more than ever before. My intention was to make Chester the most-loved, spoiled, and happy dog in the world. As a result, I've been told repeatedly that makes me a very poor disciplinarian. With gratitude to God, RMCR, and to my "Lovey" (one of Chester's 156 nicknames), I have no intention of becoming more strict.

 *James Volkman*

# "Arrr-errrr-grrr"

I had never owned a dog before, and, frankly, I hadn't really wanted one, but I knew that if I got one, it would be a Cocker, and it would be a rescue. Because my daughter, Sophie, was interested in having a dog, we adopted Max, a black Cocker Spaniel-mix, just before Christmas five years ago. He was approximately a year old at the time. Here is his story, as told by 10-year-old Sophie:

My dog, Max, is the best thing that has ever happened to me. I still remember when my mom got an email just before

Thanksgiving five years ago about RMCR finding a dog for our family. My mom had this list of ridiculous requirements we thought the rescue could never meet, but somehow, they did. Now, Max isn't just a dog; he's a member of the family.

Max has been my best friend since I laid eyes on him. In fact, when I came home from school and he was here waiting for us, I was so shocked that all I could do was scream for joy.

Max has been my constant companion ever since. When I am sad, Max lies on my bed with me for hours until I feel better. When I'm angry, Max comes and licks my face until I can't breathe. And when I'm just sitting in my bed listening to music, Max cuddles with me. He has even made friends with my guinea pigs. He sits and watches them eat their food, hoping they will spill a bit out of the cage, so he can grab it. He never barks or tries to get them; he just likes to sniff them.

Max is the smartest dog I have ever seen. He's much smarter than the expensive Labradoodle dogs all my neighbors got from breeders. We can teach Max tricks in one day. He can fetch, roll over, sit and wait, stay, give us a paw, dance, say "hamburger" (sounds like arrr-errrr-grrr), and jump over my body when I am lying on the floor. I performed all these tricks with him in the talent show when I was in fourth grade. One other smart thing he did was press his paw up against the window control to roll down the window when my mom first brought him home in the car.

Max doesn't jump up on the table when we are standing right there watching him. Instead, he patiently waits until everyone is gone, and then he jumps onto the table and eats all the leftover food.

Speaking of food, Max is obsessed with it. I remember one time when Max took six baked potatoes off the counter and hid them all over the house, with one bite out of each. Another time, Max ate a whole pot of beans and was so bloated that his stomach sagged, and he couldn't even jump up on my bed. He will do anything for food. His favorite is salmon, which gives him stinky breath, so I have to brush his teeth.

Even though Max might seem a little naughty, he is the best addition to this family, and I wouldn't trade him for the world. My mom has lost weight from walking him in the woods every day, and we all sleep better knowing he is here to protect us, from, well, the guinea pigs, the mailman, and the neighborhood dogs who poop in our front yard. I am glad we rescued him.

 *Debbie Brinley and Sophie Kontantopoulos*

# Short Tails

**Smiles Abound:** When our kids were grown, we decided to become RMCR foster parents, even though we were busy. We took in Coco and Swirl as our first fosters but quickly became foster failures. These dogs helped us through our grief when my dad passed away, and they perpetually make us smile. They are shy and timid, but despite the rough, lonely life they must have had in Missouri before being rescued, they are sweet and loving, too. Swirl, my "roley poley," spends his time making me laugh as he rolls in the grass with a big grin on his face. A natural hunting dog, Swirl loves chasing rabbits and squirrels and going for walks. Coco, my "chocolate donut," is an old mommy dog who has been through too much in her life; just this year we had to have one of her eyes removed because of cataracts. Even so, she knows her way around the house and uses the doggy door. Swirl and Coco share a special bond; she gives him kisses, and he looks after her. *-Julie Weaver*

**Pain-free:** At a year old, Melia was dropped off at a shelter in Kansas after being run over and suffering a shattered pelvis. This sweet, blonde Cocker had no problem finding another home, but her second owner also could not afford to provide her with care. As their financial distress worsened, Melia again found herself looking for a new home. RMCR had her transported to my home to be fostered. Everything about her seemed normal, but once in a while, when she was running or when I picked her up wrong, she would squeal. After RMCR paid for an operation to fix her hip and relieve her pain, Melia and I bonded through her recovery, and I knew I had to adopt her myself. Now she happily shares her life with me, my female Cocker, my male Bloodhound, and two adventurous kitties, and she no longer has any pain. *-Debbie Schriener*

# Just the Facts

**Name:** Dexi

**Nickname:** Dexidoo

**Cocker Family:** My brother, Joey

**Vitals:** Eight years old, 20 pounds

**Occupation:** Cuddlebug

**Likes:** Food, kisses, belly rubs, cuddling, being carried like a baby

**Dislikes:** Loud noises like fireworks and thunder

**Hidden Talent:** I find the most wonderful things in the trash can and in the dirty laundry hamper

**Best Things About My Brother:** Joey lets me follow him around wherever he goes, and he taught me how to drink out of the toilet.

**Most Important Lesson I've Learned so Far:** Trying to eat a pack of gum was not the best idea.

**Most Important Lesson I Should Have Learned by Now:** Going to the bathroom in the house does not make me civilized.

**If I Had Three Wishes, They Would Be:**

1. My family could cuddle with me all day long

2. The yellow snow would taste as good as the white snow

3. World peace

**Humble Beginnings:** I was rescued after being a puppy mill breeding dog for six years. I was surrendered with another puppy mill breeding dog, and my new life began.

**Medical History:** I am allergic to almost everything, even ants! I'm being treated for my allergies, but I'm still really itchy. The doctor recently found a tumor in my mammary gland, but fortunately, it was benign. I was diagnosed with heart disease, which made my mom cry, but I have many happy, healthy years ahead of me.

**Future Plans:** I plan on having many more adventures! Since leaving the puppy mill, I have discovered snow, rain, how to play with my brother, toys, car rides, and running. I can't wait to discover something else.

**One Last Thing:** For the first time, I feel happy and free. I love my family. I love my brother. I love the rescue for saving me and for finding me a real home, where I am loved.

*****

**Name:** Joey

**Nickname:** Jojo or Bubba

**Cocker Family:** My sister, Dexi

**Vitals:** Eight years old, 25 pounds

**Occupation:** Security patrol

**Likes:** Food, treats, food, belly rubs, food, my family

**Dislikes:** Strangers who walk by my car, near my house, or around anything that is mine

**Hidden Talent:** I roll down car windows, so I can stick my head out.

**Best Thing About My Sister:** Dexi doesn't tell Mom when I steal her toys.

**Most Important Lesson I've Learned so Far:** Eating a bag of chocolate cookies ends up with me in the hospital with a horrible bellyache.

**Most Important Lesson I Should Have Learned by Now:** I'm not a Great Dane.

**If I Had Three Wishes, They Would Be:**

1. All-you-can-eat restaurant for dogs

2. Dinnertime, all the time

3. People would stop putting my toys away. I place them all over the floor because that is where I want them. Stop messing with my plan.

**Humble Beginnings:** I was abandoned by my previous family after they moved. I was found in the back yard of the house after more than a week of living on my own.

**Medical History:** When I was first rescued, I was dehydrated and emaciated with ear infections in both ears, and I was infested with mites. After I was adopted, I continued to have multiple ear and eye infections. I had to have surgery to place tubes in my tear ducts because they did not drain. I haven't had an eye infection since the surgery two years ago. My ear infections cleared up after I began treatment for my allergies.

**Future Plans:** I plan on continuing my career ensuring that other people know what is mine. I hope to one day drive a car, as I'm sure I would be an excellent driver, and I would have control over all the windows. I definitely plan on staying with my current family; they adore me and, let's face it, they benefit from my diligent security detail.

**One Last Thing:** I absolutely love my family. I am grateful that I was saved by the rescue and that I was adopted by people who truly understand my value.

 *Dexi and Joey (Translated by Jennifer Clouse)*

# The Line Continues

I have owned Cockers since 1989—Max, Muffin, Maggie, Murphy, and Mollie—most of them until death. When I met my current husband, he had a Beagle named Jester, and we became a family with three dogs, two humans, and one cat. I knew Jester would outlive my aged animals, and I couldn't have that, so before the Beagle became a lone ranger, we rescued a four-month-old, tri-color Cocker from Fountain, Colorado, and renamed him Marty. Within the next few years, after watching my three aging pets go to the Bridge, we unexpectedly lost Jester to lung cancer and decided Marty, age five, would be the last animal we would own.

Marty appeared happy being king and enjoyed placing his head on my laptop while I surfed Cocker rescue websites— not because we wanted to adopt, mind you; we were simply tracking those who disappeared from the week before and celebrating them finding forever homes. We saw a picture of a brown, seven-year-old dog named Max who reappeared for many weeks. Four months after losing Jester, I candidly told my husband, "I never owned a chocolate Cocker," adding how this dog's name began with an "M"...Need I say more? I think my husband was en route to get him before I could get my shoes on.

Maxx, now a four-letter name, spent his first week showing dominance and struggling with various things. The sound of plastic grocery bags frightened him, as did shoes out of place and laundry in disarray. He wouldn't go under tables, but he knew how to use a doggie door. He walked okay on a leash and always gave an inquisitive look with his deep brown eyes and bubble-gum-colored tongue.

When I transferred Maxx's microchip, I learned it had been implanted when Bush was president. My mission was to learn of his past, which was not easy, but successful.

When his former owners and I first spoke, I could hear how my call brightened their day and now has changed both our lives. They told me they purchased Maxx and his biological sister, Molly, when the pups were eight weeks old. Six years later, these now-retired dog owners moved to a smaller house with a smaller yard and no doggie door. Molly adapted well, but Maxx, not so much. His personality changed, and he started marking inside the house. His owners worked with a trainer, but Maxx did not improve. They attempted medication recommended by their veterinarian but didn't like the lackluster behavior and personality Maxx displayed.

Not knowing what else to do, Maxx's owners drove him to the local animal shelter, but they couldn't let him go. With tears in their eyes, they took him back home. Sometime later, after Maxx attempted to bite another dog, his owners succeeded in their second attempt in taking him to the shelter.

Being in a noisy shelter and sleeping on a concrete floor didn't suit Maxx; he appeared undesirable to lookie-loos, so a shelter worker called RMCR, stating they had a dog who was "misunderstood." The rescue took him in, and then we adopted him.

His former owners still have Maxx's sister, Molly, who is solid black. We talk or exchange emails at least four or five times a month and share pictures and stories about our boy. We have a great friendship and talk about things other than Maxx's anxieties. I learned Maxx's real birth date and was recently notified when his doggie daddy died due to a spinal problem. His dad was a solid chocolate Cocker, and his mom was a Cocker-mix. Since Maxx is 17 inches at the shoulders, I wanted to know more. A DNA test revealed his ancestry includes Australian Terrier, Collie, and Malamute, and 93% Cocker Spaniel.

Almost three years after Maxx had been taken to the shelter, we arranged a reunion. Maxx recognized his owners and enjoyed a snuggle on the floor with his former human mom. Many tears were shed, but with joy, not with sadness. His former owner recently said, "My husband and I cried when we had to give him up. He was one of our babies. We were so excited to hear he found a wonderful home and a doggie-brother. Maxx definitely needs running room, and we could no longer provide that since downsizing after retirement. It was such a blessing to hear from Maxx's new owners, and it makes us feel so good knowing he found a perfect home for his needs."

My husband and I have taught Maxx a few things, like how to sit before eating dinner, "high five," and "leave it." He has taught us several things, too. For example, he loves trancing, a common Bull Terrier trait. He gets into the tomato garden no matter how Fort Knox-like we build it. His nightly neighborhood watch shift is 7:00 p.m. to 8:00 p.m., and he can do several 360-degree spins in a row to scare away anything outside the yard's concrete wall, which usually results in icing his ankle later that evening. He must have known he was taking the place of a Beagle because he breaks out in song with two hound-like howls when it's time for dinner.

Because of his height, huge white paws, and longer than normal Cocker nose, I refer to him as my baby Clydesdale/Budweiser horsie; genetics from the Malamute, perhaps? Regardless of how he came into our life, he left a loving home as a young lad and was welcomed into another as an adult.

Although Marty was okay as king, he is happier having an older brother from another mother, and we're happy to have Maxx, too.

 *A.J. Bowen and David Akers*

# Hearts Broken; Hearts Healed

Our story begins (and continues) as so many others. The loss of our beloved companion, Jessie, led us to the new love of our life, Wrigley. Hearts broken; hearts healed.

We had decided after losing Jessie that someday in the far future we would want another dog, but our hearts were so shattered that we couldn't imagine any other dog taking his place in his kingdom anytime soon. Then I started researching dog rescues and perusing the Denver Dumb Friends League website, which I like to think of as the Smart Best Friends League. That search led me to the RMCR website.

I had a special place in my heart for Cockers because my first adulthood dogs were Shelby and Zach, both Cockers. Of course,

I immediately fell in love with all the Cockers on the RMCR site but had to persuade my husband, Carl, a big dog guy, that a small dog was a good thing. After some convincing, Carl agreed to go to an adoption event to take a peek, and that's where our new dog was waiting for us, even though none of us knew it yet.

This little blonde boy with a tail and big, brown, soulful eyes was very attached to his foster mom, so it was difficult to get him away from her to walk with us. In fact, he leapt through a huge, beautiful flowerpot to get back into her lap. We appreciated his devotion and decided to make him a part of our family. I gave my husband free reign on naming him, and he settled on Wrigley, after the field where the Chicago Cubs play.

Wrigley had been found as a stray in Kansas and was in bad shape, like so many rescue dogs. Nobody knows his story, but foster care for four months turned out to be just the safe haven he needed to thrive and survive. He came to us at two years old: well-behaved, house-trained, and full of Cocker Spaniel love.

Two years later, Wrigley is the king of this castle, and we lavish him with love every day. Remember the big dog lover, Carl? He is totally wrapped around Wrigley's little paw. Wrigley is a bit spoiled, but we are over-the-moon in love with him, so it's only fitting.

We feel so fortunate to be the ones who found Wrigley, but sometimes we wonder, did he really find us? We can't help but think Jessie was behind the whole thing.

We knew nothing could ever replace the special bond we shared with Jessie for 15 years; he was our sons' "growing up" dog, my protector, and a chaser of squirrels and rabbits. But we are in love once again. The new heartbeat in our home has brought us unparalleled joy each and every day. He has healed our hearts.

 *Carl and Karen Varsolona*

# Feeling Fulfilled

When we lost our 16-year-old and 15-year-old Cocker Spaniels within three months of each other, my husband and I were devastated. We had raised them from puppies, and we considered them our children. We decided not to bring another pet into our household for a year, yet we found as the weeks went by the house just wasn't the same. We agreed it felt colder without pets, and we just couldn't get past the empty feeling every time we walked through the door. After about one month, I stumbled upon RMCR while noodling around on the Internet.

After two visits to the site, I found a picture of two Cocker sisters who could not be separated. Something spoke to me upon looking at these two cute girls, and after a couple days, I approached my husband with the picture. He contemplated the responsibility of two more dogs. We decided to meet them, and if we didn't feel good about it, we would continue to wait until the time was right.

When we were interviewed, we found out they had been abandoned and living under a house in Arkansas for 1½ years, until someone finally contacted RMCR. They had been adopted once, but the father of the family took them to a kennel and informed the personnel that RMCR would be picking them up while he and his family were on vacation. Two foster homes later, they met us.

It was love at first sight. We immediately knew the girls needed us as badly as we needed them. It took a little while to get used to their energy, as we were so accustomed to our older dogs who didn't move so quickly. We learned that Sophie is the snugglebug. She never misses the opportunity to curl up in our laps and provide abundant kisses. Chloe is the mischievous one. Now that she has overcome her shyness, she explores all over the house. We have to keep closet doors, and especially my office door, closed because she loves to get into things—especially my briefcase—and chew. We never know what she will find next. She also loves to sit with us and have her belly scratched. When we stop, she waves at us with her paw to keep scratching. This can go on forever until she falls asleep.

Don't be fooled, there were some bumps in the road in getting to know and train these girls, but when we think about where they came from, we are much more patient and tolerant. Sophie has a fear of thunderstorms, so our mailman suggested we get her a Thundershirt. She loves wearing it so much that she goes for it when she hears thunder or fireworks.

It's been six months now, and we can't imagine life without our two beautiful girls. My husband and I hope by sharing our story, others will be inspired to open their hearts and homes to a dog who needs some extra love. You will find in time that you didn't rescue them; they rescued you.

 *Nancy Krajci*

# Sweetness and Light

W
hen I heard about RMCR, I wasn't looking to adopt a Cocker. We already had three. I did, however, start volunteering for them by helping to write their newsletters.

I received a call one day from RMCR asking me if we would consider fostering because there was a Cocker at the animal shelter here in Cheyenne, Wyoming, our hometown. We agreed and went to meet Maggie at the shelter. She was so incredibly sweet. I was disturbed and saddened when they told me she had already been returned to the shelter twice for "aggression" during her short, four-year life.

When we brought her home, it took some time for her to adjust to our other three Cockers. Yes, a few fights took place. Maggie seemed anxious and uneasy, like she could never really relax. We continued to work with her and make her feel loved, while searching for someone who could provide her with a good home and give her as much love as we could. Deep inside, I subconsciously didn't want us to find anyone because I had totally fallen in love with her. When she looked into my eyes, it was as if she could see my soul.

As time went on, Maggie started to relax and get along with our other dogs. She began to trust we would accept her into our family permanently and always protect her, unlike the other homes she had been in. It was one of the happiest days of my life when my husband told me he had grown to love Maggie as well and agreed that we should adopt her.

Adopting Maggie was such a blessing to our family. It feels good to know we may have saved her life, and it made us decide that adopting is always the best way to go. There are so many wonderful, innocent, and lovable dogs out there who need a home where they are accepted, cared for, and treasured. I love the quotes "Cocker Spaniels are angels in fur coats," and "The day God created Cocker Spaniels, he sat down and smiled." I know Maggie was definitely a gift sent to us from God.

 *Jacy Olsen*

# Wisdom of the Ages

O ur happy tale begins what seems like *fur*ever ago, but was actually just four years. While expecting our second child, my very first Cocker Spaniel, Lady, whom I had since she was born, passed away from complications of old age. I was due in August and was heartbroken, but I found comfort in my other two fur babies, Avalanche and Beba. A short four days before I gave birth to our son, Avalanche passed away from a brain tumor. My husband and I were devastated; that was our second death within six weeks.

A year later, we talked about getting another Cocker, but we both decided that with a one- and three-year-old in the house, we did not want to get a puppy. I came home from work that night and searched online to see if I could find a rescue that had a Cocker Spaniel available. I found RMCR at the top of the list.

I looked at all the Cocker babies available for adoption, but one stood out to me. When I saw Silver's picture, I fell in love immediately. My husband and I both agreed he was the dog for our family and filled out the application. After what seemed like forever, the rescue approved us. We were so excited to meet our new fur-baby and take him home.

After getting Silver home and settling him in, we heard him whine in the bathroom. Our cat had cornered him in the bathtub, and he had nowhere to go! After saving Silver from the cat, we stood around laughing hysterically. Who knew the cat would be the one to scare the dog!

Next, we adopted a female Cocker Spaniel, Sissy Bear, from our local shelter. My husband and I had always agreed that adopting an older Cocker was not for us. We felt that we simply could not handle the pain of losing a fur-baby within a few years, but Sissy Bear taught us a very important lesson. We had Sissy Bear in the family for a little more than 18 months, when she was diagnosed with pancreatic cancer. We were devastated! She was only six years old, and with it having spread to her liver, the veterinarian only gave her two months to live.

Sissy Bear made it four months before passing away. We had adopted a young dog thinking we would get a good five or 10 years from her but ended up getting less than two. My husband and I realized that, even though the time we had with this young dog was cut short, we gave her the best gift she could have asked for—a forever, loving home where she was very spoiled up until the end—and in turn, we reaped the benefits of her love. She showed us that age is just a number. We learned that any amount time we could give a rescue animal was more than precious enough to make up for the pain of their loss.

I went back to looking for another Cocker and read about an older adoptable dog named Shadow on the RMCR Facebook page. My husband was at work, and I remember thinking I had to tell him about Shadow, who was definitely the dog for our family. Ironically, later in the day, my husband told me the *exact* same thing, even though we had not spoken about it yet. He had seen Shadow on the RMCR Facebook page, too! Great minds *do* think alike.

Shadow's foster family did a great job with him before we brought him into our home. Now, he really is my shadow. He always reminds us when mealtime is, and he walks so nicely on the leash that our kids have been able to walk him. We could not have asked for a better fit for the family.

As an older dog, Shadow was already potty-trained before we adopted him, and he had his adult teeth, so his chewing has been minimal. He knows he was rescued, and he loves us like no other. When the time comes again to adopt, we will look for an older dog.

 *Sarii Thomas*

# Help on the Highway

What would you name a dog who ran away and was rescued, but never seemed to learn his lesson? Scamp! I named this canine street-adventurer after the challenging offspring in *Lady and the Tramp*. This dog still wanted to jump over fences, onto counter tops, and on and over couches. He stole any food he could and found impossible gaps in fences to venture through to the unknown world.

Scamp came into my home as a foster dog when he was 1½ years old. A black-and-white, parti-color male Cocker Spaniel, his story reminded me so much of how the Disney

Scamp's life began. My Scamp found his way to RMCR in the cold of late December after having been found as a stray on a truck route in New Mexico. He was cold, dirty, and scared, wandering down the highway just before Christmas. I am told that he was wearing a filthy, little blue coat that was so stuck to his dirty, matted hair it had to be shaved off in the shelter. He spent five days in the shelter, where he was neutered. Then he was fostered by a wonderful family in Albuquerque, New Mexico, for about three weeks before he came to me in Centennial, Colorado. He had no name, so his Albuquerque family had been calling him Cody. I decided to keep the name, as it seemed fitting,

It didn't take long for me to realize I was going to have trouble with this dog still wanting to escape. Within the first few days I had him, he went missing from the back yard. As horror raced through me, I called his name, "Cody!" To my surprise and joy, he came jumping *back into* the yard, clearing the four-foot fence. I thought that would surely be the only time he would do that, but it wasn't.

After Cody disappeared three more times and repeated the jump back into the yard when his name was called, we added taller fencing inside of the fence, so he could not get over. He was jumping on and off the furniture, on and off the kitchen countertops, and on and off the patio furniture. He was so fast as he flung himself around that he appeared to be flying. That's when I realized the name Cody really didn't suit him. His desire to venture the world freely earned him the name of Scamp and the space in our home forever.

Scamp carried with him fear and aggression. He was afraid of people, and he attacked my one-year-old Cocker Spaniel,

Trusty, without provocation. I felt awful for Trusty when that happened, but with prayer, patience, and unconditional love for both dogs, I remained optimistic that we could make it work. And we did. I could have returned him to the rescue. I could have said this dog has aggression that can't be dealt with, but that could also have resulted in his life coming to an abrupt, early end, as someone else might not have been patient enough or willing to help him through his issues.

Today, Scamp and Trusty are buddies with just the occasional bossiness from Scamp because he still thinks he's top dog. I can handle sibling rivalry much better than I would have been able to handle the guilt that would have come along with giving up on Scamp.

It appears that my fostering and subsequently adopting Scamp had been God's plan, as it led me to become the foster director of RMCR. I have learned that by helping these dogs in need, I am also helping humans to heal through difficulties in their lives, which are often caused by the loss of previous Cockers. It gives me great pleasure to rehabilitate a Cocker and at the same time help a person or family move through grief that might still be hanging on from their recent losses.

Scamp and Trusty help me welcome new foster dogs into our home on a regular basis. No, Scamp is not perfect. He still gets into trouble and can frequently be heard jumping onto the kitchen counter and scavenging whatever he might find. Part of his old self still shines through as I yell, "Scamp!" and he quickly jumps down from the counter top, as if he won't be seen. He has stolen many a good sandwich and even an entire casserole. He has even been caught stealing a roast out of the crock pot and dragging it across the kitchen floor. "Scamp!" My Scamp. You have brought some trials and challenges to our home, but look at the love we share.

Since Scamp, we've had many fosters, and I became a foster failure once again with Josie, who came to me a year after Scamp as a heartworm-positive, pregnant stray from Missouri. She had nine healthy, mixed-breed puppies whom we successfully adopted out. Like Scamp, Josie never left my home.

I thought that by adopting two rescue dogs, bringing the total in my home to three Cockers, I would not be able to foster anymore. However, the longer I continued to foster, the more I understood the need to continue. I can't save every homeless dog, but I can save one or two at a time.

Still, today, when I travel the highways through New Mexico, I picture that little, black-and-white Cocker Spaniel wearing a blue coat, running lost in the cold, snowy night, hungry and afraid. I wonder if I am on the exact road where he had been found, and I know that all my efforts to rehabilitate him and the other dogs who have come through my home have been completely worthwhile.

 *Suzette Compton*

# Let the Love Shine

It was love at first sight. My now-husband had enjoyed the companionship of a Cocker Spaniel named Taffy growing up, and he knew that he would eventually want another. He found RMCR through a Google search and introduced me to the adoptable dogs posted. That was all it took. I saw a picture of this cute, red-and-white Cocker Spaniel with curly hair on her ears and a head tilt and immediately knew she was my dog.

Sunshine was a Kansas girl who had been found on the streets and transferred between places, until she found RMCR, which brought her to Colorado. She had a head tilt, limited hearing, and eye issues that took away her sight, which I would later find out were cataracts and glaucoma. She was also was a bit overweight, but none of that bothered me. Rather, it endeared me to this cute cocker.

We went through the adoption process, and Sunshine became a part of our family. She needed a lot of exercise to help her lose her excess pounds, so we got plenty of exercise together. I was surprised to find that she was a good runner. Our morning walks and runs around the park not only helped her, but they also helped me.

We made sure Sunshine had the best treatment possible, especially for her eyes. Eye appointments filled our schedules and medications for her filled our cabinets. Strangely, I find her cloudy eyes to be a beautiful color, and I was so relieved when we received the news that she would not need to have them removed.

Sunshine has shared in many of our milestones. First, she was a part of our wedding. My mother made her a special beaded collar that matched my veil. She didn't want to pose for wedding pictures, instead preferring to hide from the camera under my dress.

Sunshine also saw us through the purchase of our first home together. Since she is not able to see, it took her a while to learn the house, but once she did, she made it her own. My husband and I never question who is head of this house.

Since finding out that Sunshine is a runner, I have taken her running with me on a few 5Ks. During our first Thanksgiving 5k as a family, we were waiting to start the run when a few people in front of us looked at her and made fun of her. They mused about how there was no way she could do this race, and they unfairly judged her based on her appearance. This was not the only time someone had been surprised about her abilities, but it did stand out in my mind because of how mean-spirited their comments were. Long story short, not only did Sunshine finish the race, but she crossed the finish line running! I have the video to prove it. She really did show those naysayers the ignorance of their attitudes and proved that it's what is inside that matters.

Sunshine still has so much to share with the world. She is in the process of joining me as my furry co-therapist working with children, families, and elders. She is bursting with love for others, and she touches or melts the hearts of all she meets. On a daily basis, she demonstrates pure love, compassion, empathy, resilience, and that, despite limitations, a positive attitude goes a long way.

 *Kimberlee Bow*

# Wiggle Wiggle

W e were getting ready to go to Hawaii, so adopting another animal was not on my to-do list, but when I spotted Callie on an RMCR volunteer's lap at Petco in Lakewood, Colorado, there was just something about her eyes I couldn't resist. I then heard Callie's story. She was dropped off at an RMCR event when she was about 1½ years old. The couple had approached this same volunteer and said, "We don't want this dog," before simply handing her over.

The volunteer had only meant to help out with marketing for that particular event; she wasn't a regular RMCR volunteer, but she took a special interest in finding a good home for Callie. The rescue thought they had found such a home, and Callie's second family had her for approximately 2½ years. Every adoption contract states that adopters should return adopted dogs to the rescue if, for any reason, they cannot keep them, and that's exactly what this family did. Hence, Callie was back up for adoption. By this time, she was a matted mess, and she had an ear infection, but RMCR did what they do so well: they took care of her.

I talked to my husband, Mike, and we told the volunteer we would think about it. Mike was not thrilled about having another dog. Between our impending Hawaii vacation and the 200 critter clients we had as part of our pet sitting business, another dog didn't seem like the best idea, but we had Callie visit our home for a meet-and-greet with our dog, Daisy, and our cat, Clyde, anyway. We had lost our other dog, Lucy, to renal failure almost a year before, and Daisy was lonely. I knew Callie was missing her family every bit as much as Daisy and I missed Lucy, and I just could not turn my back on her. I told her I would be back for her, and I think she understood. The day we returned from Hawaii, we adopted Callie.

Callie has learned to get along well with our other dog, Daisy, and our daughter's two dogs, Caper and Jolie. She behaved in a hostile way toward both our daughter's dogs at first, but they quickly put her in her place. Callie can be "aggressively friendly" toward other dogs and strangers, so people often shy away from her, but a few see through her barking, and when they reach down to pet her, they find a very sweet and soft dog.

One of our biggest concerns was how Callie would interact with our grandchildren, Maya and Timmy. To our relief, Callie loves both children. She pines for them when they are not here. All we have to say is, "The kids are coming over," and she goes for the front door.

Callie is comical, agile, and smart, but she did manage to get skunked one time; the poor girl really got sprayed. With her thick Cocker coat, it took months before the smell went away.

Callie has started walking on the treadmill, which helps her burn off some of her excess energy and is especially helpful for rainy days, since she hates getting her feet wet. Perhaps that's because her feet are like four big sponges. She will do everything she can to stay on any piece of cement to avoid the wet grass when it is raining. However, she loves the snow and doesn't mind snowballs on her feet.

Callie's personality continues to emerge. We love the wiggle-wiggle she does with her little tail when she's happy. She is affectionate and enjoys stretching out for a back rub. She has learned several commands including "sit," "down," "come," "heel," and "wait for it." We are still working on "stay" and "leave it." For Callie, the third time really is the charm; she'll never find herself in need of rescue again.

 *Barbara Weitkamp*

# Short Tails

**Lady Luck:** Lady was a pretty pathetic sight when we first met her: only 17 pounds with a necessary buzz cut to remove matted hair. Her left eye had been removed because of infection. She was timid and shy, and she had us thinking back to our last Cocker Spaniel, who also had only one eye. How could we refuse her? I believe her foster mom had named her Lady because she reminded her of the character in the movie *Lady and the Tramp*. We also affectionately call her Ladybug. The first time Lady barked was at the sound of the doorbell, three months into her stay with us. That's when we knew she had finally become secure in her new home. Lady has since blossomed into a healthy, sociable, affectionate friend. She is our constant companion. She loves going to Lowe's and riding in the basket, where she gets lots of attention from shoppers and clerks. She's also an experienced traveler in our motorhome, enjoying new places, new smells, and new dogs. It's been three years since we were blessed with this little girl, and we can't imagine life without her. *-Gayle and Tom Gurksnis*

# Iron-Willed Woman

Pebbles came into our life when I thought I could become a foster parent. Really, I had the best of intentions to help a dog along her way and then let her go.

"I can take one," I said enthusiastically to the foster coordinator for RMCR. I knew fostering would take dedication and effort until the right family came along, but thinking of saving a dog's life and providing her with a temporary home filled me with great joy. Little did I know what the next two years would bring.

I went to pick up our foster baby, Pebbles, a Cocker Spaniel/Cavalier King Charles Spaniel-mix with a black mask, curly black ears, and bright, blue eyes. Pebbles had spent the first five years of her life pregnant in a steel cage. She was a spastic wreck—running around in circles, unable to stand still. I couldn't pet her for more than a second at a time. She was used to going potty in her cage at any given moment, wherever she stood, about every five minutes. A leash was a strange experience for her as was rain, snow, and affection.

I took her home, and after the first night of completing approximately 20 minutes of sleep and learning that dogs can howl as loud as a train whistle when they want your attention, I seriously wondered if I was up to the task of being a foster parent. The next day, I called the director of the rescue and asked if I could recruit the help of a behavioral specialist to learn how I could help this poor girl. I was told by the specialist, "You will probably have a hard time getting her adopted, as she is older and not the typical cute puppy that most people are looking for. And at that age, she will probably never be able to be house-trained."

"Great," I thought. "My life is over."

Being a determined soul, I wasn't going to give up. One look in Pebbles' beautiful blue eyes told me I had to forge ahead. I took her to three or four adoption events, and finally, a suitable inquiry came in from a woman in Colorado Springs. She picked Pebbles up, and after they left, I felt a horrible sadness. I cried for a solid hour. The next day, I received a call from the woman, complaining about getting approximately 20 minutes of sleep that night. She said there was no way she could keep this dog.

My heart swelled with joy as we drove down to Colorado Springs and came home with Pebbles. Now what? With more advice from the behavioral expert, we started to see some progress and finally started getting some sleep.

When I received a request to bring Pebbles to an adoption event, something inside me said, "No, I can't part with her again."

My husband, Doug, and I agreed she was part of our family. What if someone adopted her and didn't give her a proper life? No, we could not risk that happening. We filled out the paperwork, and Pebbles officially became ours.

After a week of teaching Pebbles how to use a staircase and how to climb up on a curb, which her back legs were too weak to do, we noticed a terrible cough developing. We went off to the veterinarian for a check-up, and X-rays revealed a mass on her lung that was most likely cancer. My heart sank. It couldn't be cancer! But two oncologists confirmed the diagnosis. I immediately contacted a reputable veterinary hospital, and after multiple consultations and further testing, they said they would have to remove a third of her left lung.

We were horrified. I sobbed uncontrollably, and prayed my heart out for this dear, sweet, little angel to survive this very risky operation, even though they told me her chances of surviving it were questionable at best. To our incredible relief, Pebbles pulled though and proved that after what she had been through in her life, she had developed an iron will to survive. She was destined to be ours after all.

Five years later, a consistent potty-training routine has made Pebbles fully house-trained. She has learned many words, including "sit," "walkies," "carrot treat," "nite-nite," "outside," and "kisses for the mom." The most hysterical one of all, "teeth," causes her to produce an adorable toothy smile! She also has learned how to play tug-of-war with her favorite toy, an old wool hat she fetches. She has become affectionate and will cuddle up next to us on the couch, especially when there is a thunderstorm. She has learned to sleep through the night and will usually wake us exactly five minutes before the alarm.

I realized a very important lesson from my experience with Pebbles: I don't have what it takes to be a foster mom, at least not for Pebbles. She was meant to be part of our family. We couldn't be more proud of our little girl; she has turned out to be the smartest, sweetest, and bravest dog that we could have ever hoped for. And she has proved to us angels really do exist!

 *Jeanette Salzburg*

# Springing Spaniel

Charley became a part of our lives a year ago. Her foster mom, Debbie, brought her over to meet us on a Thursday evening, during the season opener for the Broncos. It was a sacrifice for us all, but such a good one! We adopted Charley that night, and she has blessed us continually since then. At six years old, she is funny and spunky, making us laugh all the time.

Shortly after we got Charley, we went to Vail to celebrate our anniversary and stayed at a beautiful hotel that allowed pets. She drew a lot of attention as she wore her favorite sweater around town. At one point, we came around a corner, and Charley jumped right up and sat down on a chair made from skis. What a photo that was! Later, she entertained diners when she jumped up on a three-foot-high stone wall in front of a restaurant and walked along it. We all had a good laugh at that. Charley jumps up on every wall, and even on large stones, while she's out walking. She really enjoys her gymnastic moves.

Charley's other favorite pastime is playing with her stuffed animal friends. We keep them in a basket, and when I say, "Go get your duck (or monkey, or gingerbread man)," she runs over to the basket and gets exactly what I requested. She then runs back with it, and it becomes my job to tug on it while she growls and tugs back. Then, I tell her to let it go, which she does. I throw it, and she chases it, growling the whole time. She brings it back to me, and we start over. I have taught her to wait until I count to three. Then I throw it straight up in the air, and she catches it in her mouth!

She taught herself how to roll over after she saw her foster mom's dogs do it for a treat. She still does it as a trick to get a treat, and although she isn't very graceful at it, she's most certainly enthusiastic. She completes her roll, sits up, and looks at me like, "Didn't I do a good roll, Mom?"

Charley has filled a void in our lives caused by the loss of our beloved Cocker Spaniel, Chloe, last July. She is affectionate, loyal, and bonded to me and my husband equally. She loves our extended family, too. She goes everywhere with us, including on a tour bus in Deadwood, South Dakota, this summer. Nothing quite compares to the greeting she gives us when we get home and walk through the door. She literally stands up on her back legs and leans into my legs and hugs me. Life wouldn't be the same without her.

 *Kimberly Conboy*

# Our South Paw

W e had had three Cockers for a number of years, but the passage of time meant that Madison was now an only dog. After the passing of her buddy, we spoiled Madison for several weeks and lavished attention on her, but we knew we needed to get her a companion. She was 12 years old, and although she was a very young 12, she needed a friend to keep her going.

We set out to attend an adoption event where we could meet some Cockers. We had adopted several older dogs throughout the years, and young dogs and puppies did not interest us. Our new friend would also have to be female—we had always had female dogs—but aside from that, we really didn't have any strict parameters. Of course, we brought Madison along so that she could help us choose her new "sibling."

There were several Cockers at the adoption event, all different sizes, colors, and ages. Trying to choose just one was rather overwhelming, to say the least. All our previous fur-kids had been foster dogs in our home for some time prior to their official adoption. It had always gone something like this:

Me to my husband: "I'm going to drop off Madison today with the rescue folks."

My Husband to me: "Why are you doing that? I thought we were keeping her."

Me: "Oh, yes, okay. I'll let them know."

And so it went.

This time, we sat there observing the dogs we had just met, offering pats and kind words and chatting with the rescue folks. I wondered how we would make such an important decision. What if we chose the wrong dog? They all needed homes!

Finally, we noticed that Madison had taken an interest in a young male (the horror!) named Sundance. She was sniffing him up and down as he just sat there. He was very laid back and rather unconcerned about Madison's pushy, bossy demeanor. She was in charge, and he seemed to recognize that, but it didn't bother him. Finally, after a full and thorough sniffing, Madison sat down. Had she made her choice? Sundance was barely a year old; it seemed a shame for us to adopt such a young pup when we were more than willing, even preferring, to adopt an older dog. But then, Sundance had been in foster care for a few months. Such a young dog...why had nobody adopted him yet? What was wrong with him, we wondered?

We asked if we could take Sundance outside for a walk in the field with Madison. Of course, that was no problem. While walking the pair, my husband talked about what we should do. For my husband, it was pretty straightforward. There was nothing more to ponder; we were going to take Sundance home. Didn't I agree? Well, yes, I think so...

And with that, we had our new dog.

Today, Sundance and Madison are two of the most bonded dogs I have ever seen. Their connection with each other is especially interesting since they didn't grow up together, and there is an 11-year age difference between the two. They snuggle together and groom each other. Sundance often uses Madison as his pillow, resting his head on her back. When he needs some reassuring grooming, he parks himself near her and waits. If she doesn't notice his need within a minute or two, he gives her a nudge with his butt, as if to say, "Hey, I'm waiting!" Madison always dutifully gets to work, licking his back, his ears, and his head. This gives Sundance such a look of contentment on his face; I am certain there is nowhere else he'd rather be at that moment.

Sundance is a big snuggle bug with his humans, too. He loves attention, kisses, and pats. There is no such thing as too much attention for Sundance. He won't hesitate to let you know with his left paw (he's a lefty) that he'd like some more loving. And he never hesitates to try to groom his humans the way Madison grooms him. He has a special fondness for my husband's hair-challenged head.

We don't know much about Sundance's time prior to being taken into rescue. He was found as a stray roaming the streets when he was only several months old. Our hearts break when we think about his cold, lonely, uncertain start in life, but it was the start that brought him to our family, the exact place he was meant to be. All these years later, I now realize that of course no one had adopted him; he was waiting for us!

 *Kelly Mullins*

# On Top of the World...
## and the Table, and the Counter

O ur aging Cocker Spaniel, Samantha, was such a wonderful dog that when we decided to add a new Cocker to our family a year after the loss of our previous male, we enlisted her help in training him. We looked online for a few months for a male Cocker Spaniel who resembled our previous dog, Stewie. Finally, we stumbled across the RMCR website and saw a picture of Max.

We inquired about Max and arranged to meet him and his foster mom, Christina, at Petco in Golden, Colorado. When we saw Christina rolling into the parking lot with Max's head poking out the window and his ears blowing in the breeze, we could both tell he had swagger. When Christina brought Max out of the car, I started to cry because he reminded me so much of Stewie. He had style and naughtiness all rolled in to a streamlined little body.

Christina informed us that Max loves to jump on everything. I thought, how could this dog possibly jump on things that greatly exceeded his size? When we got him home, I had my answer. There was nothing he couldn't jump on! I found him on top of our dining room table, with all the chairs pushed in, on the kitchen counter, on couches, and on beds. You name it; he was either jumping on it or climbing on it.

This little dog could even counter surf! Nothing was safe on the kitchen counters for the first year we had him. He climbed on a chair, then onto a bar stool, and then onto the kitchen counter. It didn't matter if the chairs and stools were pushed in; he would push them out in order to get a good footing, so he could access crumbs, hotdog buns, cookies, and once, a whole papaya complete with seeds! For a while, I thought maybe Max was just hungry, so I pumped up his meal portions twice daily. That didn't curtail his counter surfing. At least his pursuit was athletic: within the first month, Max's back muscles looked like a six-pack from all the jumping.

Max was on the go all the time. My husband occasionally made the mistake of letting him off-leash, and he would take off. If he wasn't down the street in the neighbor's garage searching for squeaky toys, he was jumping in the cab of the garbage truck every Tuesday morning or jumping through the window of the USPS mail carrier's Subaru, ready to take a ride.

It was believed that Max's previous owner had been put into a nursing home, and during his first year with us, Max seemed to continuously search for him. I could tell it was going to be a while before he felt like we were his family because he was so confused by what had happened to him, but it did happen over time. He's been with us 2½ years now, and he has turned into a companion. He has calmed down and now realizes he has a safe, stable, loving home where the toys, tennis balls and treats flow freely.

We love our Max. He brings a smile to the face of everyone he meets. Our neighbor's children fight to walk him during the summer months because he is so much fun to be around.

 *Lisa Boulay & Rodney Bradford*

# Down the Rabbit Hole

'There's a concrete slab under here!" My husband, Don, had been busy with the chainsaw tearing apart our beautiful deck because I thought, just maybe, I had heard my dog whimpering under there.

We had adopted Jasper four years earlier after he was mistreated and starved, with almost no human interaction. RMCR thought since we had a fairly quiet household with no children at home, we might be a good match for the timid, little waif.

They were right. We love our floppy-eared, freckled, happy-go-lucky dog, with his perpetual smile. But now, he was missing. When our other adopted Cocker, Keisha, answered our call that early spring afternoon and came inside with no Jasper, we looked all over the back yard. No Jasper. I called and called. No Jasper. We have a secure back yard, but I thought he must have gotten out somehow. We checked with every neighbor and walked miles calling his name, but no Jasper. Needless to say, we were worried. We lived in a new neighborhood, with which Jasper wasn't particularly familiar. The neighborhood was surrounded by green space with frequent reports of nearby predators. We spent a restless night getting up several times to check outside and call quietly, hoping Jasper had returned.

The next morning, I brewed some coffee, and, standing on the deck with my cup in hand, tried calling Jasper once again. I thought maybe, just maybe, I heard a dog whimper. I called again, and it seemed that the soft whimpering was coming from under my feet. I called Don, and he started ripping apart the deck, which stood about 2½ feet above the level of the surrounding yard and had redwood lattice enclosing its bottom portion. Don tore out the lattice but couldn't see Jasper. Then, he tore up a bit of the flooring, and said, "There's a slab under here; an old patio."

After some more deconstruction, he discovered a small hole at the side of the old ground-level patio. "I think the rabbits have been digging a hole under here. You don't suppose he got in there?"

The beauty of our surrounding green space comes with a small problem. Well, really, many small problems: rabbits. Many, many little cottontails. It seems we found a rabbit nest, and we couldn't help but wonder if Jasper had found it, too.

Our son, Rich, came to help because the rescue effort was turning into a major piece of work. In order to make room to dig, more of the deck had to be ripped out. When they cut a large opening in the deck floor, they had to remove crossbeams, and only then could the digging begin. Don and Rich took turns digging for more than two hours, looking for a dog I thought I might have heard whimper. I frantically called veterinarians, trying to find one who would accept a dog I was sure would be cold, dehydrated, and possibly injured. After an eternity, Rich shined a flashlight into the hole and said, "Wait, I think I see him!"

Jasper was there, but he was silent. That couldn't be a good thing.

Finally, after digging a tunnel about five feet long, Rich was able to grab hold of Jasper's back leg and inch him out. Free at last!

And Jasper's condition? Well, he shook himself off, got a drink of water and ran off to play. After more than 24 hours of being stuck in a rabbit warren—alone and hungry, in the dark—he just wanted to play. Of course, Jasper couldn't understand the trouble his loving father and brother had gone through to save his life, but then, he's a dog.

Don and I stood looking at the jagged remains of what had been a very attractive deck and discussed rebuilding it. The problem was that we just couldn't figure how to fortify a raised deck so the burrow-digging bunnies and curious Cocker Spaniels couldn't get under it.

Now, we're building a redesigned patio at ground level, with no areas that are out of sight to tempt the bunnies. And we hope to continue enjoying our floppy-eared, freckle-faced, clever little Cocker Spaniel for many, many more years—above ground!

 *Cheryl Cadwallader*

# A Gift from My Sister

**M**aggie and I have grieved together since losing my sister, her owner, two years ago. Because we worked through our grief together, we have become a bonded duo. Poor Maggie has had a lot of losses in her 10 years, but now I think she realizes that she is not alone, and her permanent home is with me.

Maggie had been rescued by a Cocker rescue in Virginia as a pup. She spent two years in an apartment with her owner, but when that owner passed away, she went back to the Cocker rescue in Virginia. That's when my sister, Sheila, had found her and added her to her family, which already included another buff Cocker Spaniel named Mollie. Maggie and Mollie became real sisters, and they were just adorable together, until Mollie passed away in January 2012, and my sister followed in July later that year.

I stayed with Maggie during my sister's funeral, and we consoled each other that week. As I packed my bag to leave, Maggie turned her back to me and then proceeded to chew up everything in the suitcase, when I left it open and unattended. She was truly grieving and angry I was leaving, too.

Maggie lived with my nephews for a couple of months but had a difficult time adapting in their homes. I knew I needed her as much as she needed me, so I flew back to Virginia and picked up Maggie to bring her home to Colorado. Maggie did not like being outside in the rain or snow. She picked her way across the lawn as if the grass were foreign to her. Each day was a new adventure of chasing bunnies, battling a large buck, and tangling with oak bushes.

At 10 years old, Maggie is now well-adjusted and trusting. She is attending an obedience class with other dogs to help with her socialization and to remedy some protection issues. She follows me everywhere, and she is now comfortable taking long walks and even runs with me.

Together, we still miss Sheila every day, and there have been times over the past two years I have seen Maggie with what appears to be tears in her eyes, tears I attribute to her sadness over Sheila's passing. We have helped each other in this journey; Maggie is the greatest gift my sister could have ever left for me.

*Michelle Hektor*

# House Filled with Love

Months had gone by, and I still found myself walking around the house looking for Sophie, my beloved Great Pyrenees who had passed away. The house was quiet now that she was gone, and it surprised me that I missed her so much. It is so hard to outlive your friend.

When my wife and I began thinking about getting another dog, something a little smaller, a patient at my wife's workplace suggested RMCR, a group whose name brought me back to fond remembrances of a Cocker Spaniel I had as a little boy. I looked at the rescue website, and a little, blond Cocker named Farrah caught my eye. She was listed as a courtesy for her mom, who had to give her up, but when I called and set up a time to meet Farrah, I found that her mom was simply not ready to let her go. I could only imagine the difficulty she faced.

After a couple weeks, Farrah's mom finally realized the time had come to give up her dog. I spoke with her on the phone in order to reassure her that her little Cocker was going to a good home, and we set up a time to get her. Farrah seemed a little timid at first but warmed up to us in just a couple days.

My wife was hoping for a dog who would appreciate the acre of land we live on, and indeed, Farrah does. When she first stepped foot in our yard, it was as if she had never been off-leash before. To this day, she runs and runs with her little head on the ground sniffing as she goes. I don't know how she does it, but we will be looking for her in one direction, and she will come racing up behind us, blowing by at great speed, sounding like a heard of horses.

Farrah is, without a doubt, the most affectionate dog I've ever met. When we sit on the porch swing, Farrah leaps into the spot between us with great abandon in order to snuggle up. Moreover, when she seems to be asleep on the floor, I just look at her, and her stub of a tail starts to wag.

Farrah has been with us for five years now. When I come home late, she's waiting for me (and for her dog cookie, of course). When my wife had surgery, Farrah was there to help her heal. Life brings sadness sometimes, but Farrah mends our broken hearts. Her loving presence is felt throughout the house. When I drop her off at the groomer, I find myself missing her, even though it's for just a few hours.

I love the quirky things she does, like snapping at the vacuum and leaping onto the bed while we're trying to make it. Furthermore, once we do get the bed made, she makes sure it is right by flipping upside down and wiggling all over it. I can only guess she thinks the bed being made must be her cue to play. If I scold her, she just looks at me and wags her tail. Oh, and did I mention she watches Broncos football? All in all, little Farrah has made our life quite a bit more wonderful.

 *Mike Kirby*

# Short Tails

**Miss-chief:** Four-year-old Molly Monster, Molly Mischief, Molly Monkey or Molly Munchkin (among other names) is a great example of how love can change any life. In the beginning, Molly was shy and insecure; her eyes were vacant and empty. That didn't last long after she found her new home and got the love and care she needed, along with the guidance of a private trainer. Nowadays, this smart, strong-willed, independent dog always wants to be close and loving, especially at night. And in the morning, she gives me gentle, tiny licks on my arm or face to tell me she is ready to go outside. She's got the energy of a puppy, and she absolutely loves her ball, playing her own version of hide-and-seek by hiding it somewhere she can't reach it. She then stands and voices her displeasure until I get down on my hands and knees and retrieve it for her. How far Molly has come is absolutely amazing. She is simply a different dog. She doesn't make friends easily but once she does, look out. She will be in your lap squealing, kissing, and loving you. -*Sally Hardwick*

D awn had a Cocker Spaniel named Izzy, whom she purchased while in college. Izzy was there for Dawn through many big life events: her young adult life, her college years, her move to Colorado from North Dakota, her marriage to Chuck, and the birth of their daughter, Emerson. From the day that Emerson came home from the hospital, Izzy bonded with her. The two were together constantly, and they became the best of friends as Emerson grew up.

Emerson's bond with Izzy became even more important when Dawn was diagnosed with breast cancer at age 30.

This time, Izzy was not only there for Dawn, but she was there for the entire family and helped them all get through that difficult time.

Sadly, Izzy passed away from old age four years ago. Emerson was only five at the time, and she took Izzy's passing extremely hard. Chuck and Dawn tried to replace Izzy with a new puppy, Molly, a Cavalier King Charles Spaniel. Molly was extremely sweet, but it turned out she was a one-person dog, and that one person was Dawn.

Emerson struggled to understand why this new puppy did not like her as much as Izzy had. Three years passed after Izzy left the family, and Emerson still talked about her all the time. Anytime she drew pictures of the family, she included Izzy in them. People would question why there were always two dogs drawn in Emerson's pictures, and she would say, "This dog is Izzy. She was my best friend, and she died."

Of course, this was heartbreaking to Dawn and Chuck, so they decided to get another Cocker Spaniel. They found RMCR and applied for adoption. While they waited to be approved, Dawn and Emerson spent countless hours looking at pictures and reading biographies on the available dogs. They found several who interested them, but most had already been placed by the time they were approved. Then, a volunteer suggested Coco, who had yet to be posted to the website. She was a chocolate-colored dog who had just been rescued from another state. Her daughter, Chanel, had already been adopted, but Coco still needed a good home. Dawn arranged to meet Coco in a few days.

It was believed that Coco was a puppy mill momma. She had just turned two but had already had four litters. During her final pregnancy, Coco was in labor for several days, and when she only produced one puppy, her owner dropped her and her puppy off at a shelter. A few days later, Coco started having health issues, which turned out to be from a miscarried puppy that she had not expelled. The shelter took care of that issue and also spayed her, and then they transferred Coco and her puppy to RMCR.

After reading her story, Dawn felt excited about meeting Coco but also troubled by her horrible past. Dawn knew that she and her family could give Coco a good home and more attention than she almost certainly had ever had. Dawn expressed to a friend that she was sad that Coco and Chanel could not be placed in the same house, and within 30 minutes of that conversation, she received a call from an RMCR volunteer stating that the person adopting Chanel had backed out, and the puppy was now up for adoption. She mentioned that the family could have first dibs on the puppy if they wanted Chanel instead of Coco. Dawn said that she would discuss it with her family and get back to them.

As Dawn thought it through, she began to feel that these events did not happen by accident. She had a strong sense her family was being pointed in the direction of adopting both dogs. When Chuck came home, they had a family discussion. Although Chuck and Emmy needed little convincing about the puppy, the family decided they would meet both dogs, and if everything went okay, they would adopt both.

They met the dogs a few days later, when Chanel was seven or eight weeks old. She was spunky, and she warmed up to the family right away. As for Coco, she turned out to be wonderfully sweet. She was protective of her puppy but nuzzled the family members affectionately with her nose. They could tell she just wanted to be petted and loved. It was an easy decision for the family to adopt both dogs.

Coco and Chanel came to live in their forever home the weekend after Thanksgiving. Molly did not like the new dogs, and they did not like her. Additionally, Coco had some health issues, so the family spent a lot of time at the veterinarian's office. While Coco's condition improved, Molly warmed up to Chanel. Soon, they started playing together all the time, and over time, Molly and Coco got friendly as well. Now, nine months later, Molly, Coco, and Chanel are all friends.

Both Coco and Chanel love hanging out with Molly and Dawn during the day. It's a great situation for all the dogs since Dawn has a job where she is able to work from home. Coco and Molly are definitely Dawn's dogs; they follow her everywhere. But Dawn and Chuck also got what they wished for: the puppy developed a strong bond with Emerson. Now, they are inseparable: sleeping together, playing together, and watching TV together. Emerson mentions Izzy less and less. She is now happy with all three dogs and has a special place in her heart for them. Molly is still the princess, while Coco is the gentle sweetheart. Chanel is the spunky comedian, with beautiful eyelashes that are about an inch long. It seems that her name was perfect for her!

Of course, no dog will take the place of Izzy for Emerson, but at least Emerson is able to make happy memories with her new best friend. As an added bonus, Coco and Chanel were able to stay together, and the house feels like a home with its three wonderful pups.

 *Dawn Wittenberg*

# The Perfect Temperament

Gentleness, kindness, and caring entered my life in the form of a parti-colored, rescued Cocker Spaniel named Trixie. When I first saw her on the RMCR website, I immediately called my wife over to share a look at this beautiful dog. Within the week, I completed the adoption application, tidied the house for our home visit from Trixie's foster mom, and welcomed Trixie into our home.

Trixie was rescued from a puppy mill. She had been a breeding dog, and it seemed she was used to being still and not having control over her life situation. This provided her with a very accepting attitude. She was willing to be picked up and held at any time and seemed to appreciate any attention she received.

Our new pet brought out kindness in those around her. One time, we had a party at our home with two very young children present. The children were drawn to Trixie as she lay on the couch, but instead of the usual roughhousing manner children tend to exhibit toward dogs, they were naturally tender with her. Good parenting combined with a gentle-spirited dog helped to create a wonderful evening for all.

Trixie's demeanor inspired me to seek information about animal behavior therapy, so she could participate in some basic command training and be tested by a qualified veterinarian for behavior and attitude. I knew she would do fine with the veterinarian and looked forward to our visit, but when the veterinary assistant said she would take Trixie back for her test, I felt like a father sending my child into kindergarten for the first time. I was so relieved when Trixie appeared a short while later having passed with flying colors. Now, as a therapy dog, she visits patients and staff at Porter Adventist Hospital weekly.

Trixie is a wonderful addition to our household. She gets along well with our other Cocker Spaniel and with our family and friends. Her gentle demeanor affects my wife and me when she joins one of us on our laps or simply lies calmly on the ottoman. Trixie is calm, and now, so are we.

 *Ron and Mary Shuster*

# Winter Sun

It all started with Wesley, who came from a rescue in Alamosa, Colorado. It didn't take him long to completely win our hearts and make us wonder how our lives had ever been complete without a Cocker.

This caused me to start researching Cocker rescues, which led to us becoming foster parents for RMCR, albeit briefly. Our first foster followed Wesley's lead and stole our hearts immediately, so we adopted her. Now we had "his" and "hers" Cockers.

After a couple of months, we decided to foster again. We took in two more fosters from the rescue, Snowcone and Dipper. Dipper was a young, healthy boy who found a forever family quickly. My poor little Snow, however, had too many health concerns for most people to overlook. At 13 years old, she is deaf and toothless, and she has mammary tumors. Despite all that, she shines like the snow on a sunny day, and her presence warms our hearts.

We knew we had to keep Snow and love her always, so now we have three adorable, sweet Cocker Spaniels sharing our lives and making our home extra cozy. Each has his or her own special qualities. Wesley is a hopeless momma's boy who is never far from me. If I am separated from Dipper, and my husband wants to know where I am, he just tells Wesley, "Find mommy." Wes puts his nose to the ground, and off he goes to find me.

Lucy is like a cuddly toy. She adores having Daddy scratch her face, ears, and tummy. She expects this every morning before the day gets started.

Little Snow is the hall monitor. She tattles on the cats every chance she gets. This old gal isn't about to be left out of any activities, but, not surprisingly, she's also a cuddle bug— cuddling is one of the many things Cockers do best.

Coming home from work to three excited Cocker faces dancing around me makes anything that may have gone awry earlier in the day disappear. They are joyful little souls that bring happiness and cuddles everywhere they go. We love our Cocker Spaniels; with them blessing our home, our lives feel complete.

 *Deborah Striegel*

# Ear Glider

When Red Rock Canyon Park first opened in Colorado Springs, Colorado, my daughter-in-law, Wendy, and I decided to take 14-year-old Toby to do some exploring of the new park. We climbed up the mountain path and were almost to the top, when Toby wanted to get off-leash. With no other hikers in sight, I decided to let him go and sniff around.

Before I could turn around, a huge bird flew overhead. Toby took off after it with his eyes focused only on the sky. It flew over the canyon wall, and Toby "flew" off right behind it. My heart stopped as I saw him fly into the air and then disappear.

Wendy and I dashed to the edge of the cliff but couldn't see Toby anywhere. All we saw was the canyon floor more than 30 feet below, straight down a sheer cliff. There were no outcropping or trees, and there was no Toby.

I started to cry, thinking he was dead, as we searched for the quickest safe passageway down the cliff. We began backtracking to the entrance of the park, so we could make our way down to the canyon floor, and I constantly called Toby's name. Suddenly, we heard a rustling in the scrub oak bushes nearby, and up from the edge of the canyon came Toby!

Toby's excitement made it seem like he was eager to tell us about his adventure. We quickly checked him over and found him in perfect condition. How could that be?

Toby's safe return will always be a mystery to us. Wendy and I both know with certainty that we saw him fly off that cliff. All we can think is that maybe it was his long Cocker ears that allowed him to glide to safety.

 *Mary Walis*

# Perfect Timing

W e had adopted two Cocker Spaniels prior to Ray, although neither is still with us today. We got Otto, our first, at an adoption fair when he was about six weeks old. He was an all-black, purebred Cocker, who turned out to be an alpha. He taught us that with patience and consistency, we could get past his stubbornness.

When Otto was about eight years old, we got another Cocker, Grizz, from the local humane society. He was five months old and had no training whatsoever. He came from a neglectful place and was scared of everything, but our love and patience allowed us to help him move beyond his past.

Otto and Grizz soon became inseparable. They went to the park and to doggy daycare together. They both loved their birthday parties and opening their presents on Christmas morning. Otto was with us until just short of his 16th birthday, and Grizz lived another four years until his 11th birthday, when he became very ill.

After watching Grizz pass on so young, we struggled with the idea of getting another dog. We knew there would be a third stocking hanging from the mantle at Christmas someday, but we didn't talk about it much. It was just too painful.

A few months ago, my wife, Dee, started talking about adoption. I still wasn't ready, but she was, which put us at somewhat of an impasse. Dee learned about RMCR and soon started volunteering. We even signed up as short-term fosters, which seemed like a reasonable solution for the time being.

Dee picked up our first foster, Ray, on a Friday night, and he took right to her. He followed her around, sat on her lap, and refused to leave her side. I met him later that night when I got home, and we proceeded to get acquainted. He was easy-going and parti-colored, just what I wanted in our next dog.

Dee took him to an adoption fair the next day. I knew she was already falling in love with him only after one night in the house, and I, too, was starting to feel an attraction. I thought I wasn't ready to be a doggy daddy again, but Ray had me questioning my resolve, so I sent Dee a text while she was at the event and told her if she was feeling like he is the right one for us, I was on board to keep him.

Our adoption went through, and Ray officially became ours. He has since brought lightheartedness back into our house. We walk him in the nearby park every morning before we go to work, and he loves it, although it still seems like it's a new experience to him. He gets excited when we put his walking harness on him, as if he knows what is about to happen (I think he does). He loves to meet new people and their puppies. He's learning new things and has more to learn, but he does everything with an eager enthusiasm.

I know Ray came to us by design. We were ready for a new dog, even though one of us wasn't aware of it. Ray's previous owner surrendered him to RMCR just a few days before we became foster parents. Everything fell into place perfectly; if we could have hand-picked our next dog, it would have been Ray. My only regret is that Ray didn't get to meet Otto and Grizz. They would all have gotten along and been the best of friends, but then we would have needed to get a bigger bed.

 *Scott and Dee Walker*

# My First Foster

A s soon as Cinnamon walked into my back yard, I knew something was wrong. She squatted to go potty every five steps, and her ears dragged on the ground. I sat watching her, and every once in a while she came by to look at me. With each lap she moved a little closer, but when I reached out to her, she cowered and walked away. She constantly paced the yard.

This was our first day fostering a dog. We had our own dog, Midnight, to whom Cinnamon easily related, so we used that to help Cinnamon become more comfortable with us. We showed kindness to Midnight, of course, and talked softly to Cinnamon. Still, when she came in the house, she shook with nervousness the entire time.

Cinnamon had been removed from a neglectful family by animal control. Marks on her knees from lying on cement in all temperatures remained even after RMCR took her in; they were a constant reminder of her previous outdoor life.

The next day, RMCR took her to the veterinarian for an intake exam and grooming. Cinnamon came back shaved; she looked like a brand new dog, and she exuded more confidence. Unfortunately, she was found to have a bladder infection, and the veterinarian noticed some recent slashes on her stomach, which he reported to animal control. An animal control officer came to my house to take another look at Cinnamon and photograph the marks for evidence. They returned to my home periodically a few more times to check on her.

To help her learn to accept affection, my husband encouraged me to put Cinnamon near us on the couch. To make the experience of being picked up and put on the couch less traumatic, I covered Cinnamon in a blanket first. She shook the first few times I did this, but after a week or so, Cinnamon sat on the couch and let me pet her! The first time she relaxed enough to fall asleep on the couch brought tears to my eyes. She was really starting to trust us.

One night we noticed that Cinnamon's stomach seemed to be getting larger, as if she were pregnant, but that couldn't be possible—she was 15 years old. My husband and I took her to the veterinarian, and after a biopsy, we learned it was an incurable, fast-growing cancer. The rescue made the hard decision to let Cinnamon go to the Rainbow Bridge.

Although letting our first foster dog go wasn't easy, we take solace knowing our family gave Cinnamon the opportunity to enjoy the final weeks of her life. To this day, four years later, we continue to foster for RMCR. Because we opened our door and our hearts to Cinnamon, she learned about trust, love, and comfort; she experienced the good life every dog should have. Fostering allows us to help displaced dogs find this happiness again and again.

 *Debbie Cole*

# No Moe Medicine

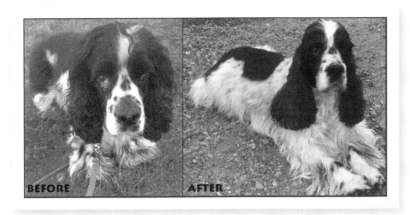

BEFORE     AFTER

"Moe is an 8-yr-old intact male Cocker Spaniel. Registered, but cannot find his papers. Has a cherry eye, lives outside, hasn't been groomed in a year. He is the sweetest... call Rebecca, $75.00."

***

After responding to the online ad, I arrived to find a camper-trailer sitting on a large, junkyard-looking, dirt lot in the country. There were some goats, a few chickens, and one horse. Rebecca came out of the trailer and walked me over to the split rail fencing. At one end of a 25-foot chain was Moe, a black-and-white Cocker; the other end was attached to a dog house. Moe had a bubble-gum colored blister inside the bottom of one eye. A black spaghetti strand of hair constantly fell from his head in between his eyes. He didn't appear to have a tail, and his hair was dry and flaky. Flies were constantly landing on his moist, scabbed nose.

After a few minutes, a black herding dog appeared, and Rebecca let Moe off the chain. Moe enjoyed following the other dog, but Rebecca told me Moe could possibly run too far, so we had to keep an eye on him while she filled out the relinquishment paperwork. She said Moe was about eight or nine years old; she would get me his AKC paperwork another time, as it was in storage. She was sad to see him go, but Rebecca's daughter convinced her to find Moe a home where he could be indoors as summer was coming to an end. She knew Moe didn't belong at the end of that heavy chain anymore.

I asked what kind of food he ate, and Rebecca told me, "At times he wouldn't eat the dog food I gave him. I would see him carrying his empty food bowl around, but he eventually ate the food he spilled on the ground. Occasionally, I would give him a special treat by tossing out a pizza crust to him."

Moe and I drove off to spend a few hours together. He tolerated his bath and was very patient when I shaved all his hair. I did find a tail, but it wasn't much. His toenails were long and curved, with a few touching the pads on his paws. After Moe's coat was dry, I allowed him to play in the back yard with my two male Cockers, Maxx and Marty. Moe appeared to walk a bit bow-legged; I figured this was due to the chain weighing him down under his chest and between his front legs. He slowly followed my dogs into the house, but when his paws touched the carpet, he stopped and ran back outside. I realized he had never touched carpet, and it must have scared him. A few minutes later, we drove one hour to admit him as a new RMCR foster. After arriving to his new foster home, he was quickly approached by other Cocker Spaniels, but his social skills were superb, and I knew he would be safe.

Four days later, a veterinarian noted many abnormalities: slight hair loss, pink skin, muscle atrophy, skin bacteria, ear yeast, nose infection, dry skin/fleas, tail wound, shoulder mass, and clostridial enteritis (intestinal infection). He was also six pounds underweight.

Moe was a very calm dog. He didn't get excited about much, and he was eager to please. He got along with every creature, two- or four-legged. With such a great personality and an adorable coat coloring, he quickly became an excellent representative of the rescue and the breed. During an RMCR marketing event, a family with three young children fell in love with Moe and noticed the red bump in his eye. A rescue volunteer explained cherry eye to the children, noting it was an issue with his gland that required surgery to correct. The children donated their allowance money to the rescue, stating the entire $10 was specifically to have Moe's eye fixed.

During the next few months, Moe had his teeth cleaned, his cherry eye repaired, and the mass on his shoulder removed. His nose scab healed, and his skin became less itchy. Moe continued to experience intestinal problems, which was eventually diagnosed as canine protein-losing enteropathy (PLE), a relative of irritable bowel disease.

Just when the veterinarian thought Moe's diet and medications were working, Moe had a relapse, and things didn't look good. I started driving an hour each way to join Moe's foster mom at his weekly veterinary appointments. IIis prescription kibble and nearly a dozen daily doses of supplements and medications started to pay off, and a few weeks later, his protein levels were finally stable, although not within acceptable levels. The veterinarian told us both, "It is time to make Moe comfortable."

The meaning of this statement was devastating, and we feared Moe would not be with us for long. A few days later, Moe moved into my home and enjoyed following his two foster brothers, Maxx and Marty, although he moved a bit slower than them.

I searched the Internet and found several support sites, blogs, and others postings of people's experiences with canine PLE. People talked about diets that worked for their canines, and with this new information, I worked alongside Moe's previous foster mom and veterinarian to improve Moe's health. Within two weeks, his protein levels improved. Four weeks later, his protein was finally in the normal range. Ten weeks later, we were able to begin decreasing his medications. He started running more often, keeping pace with his foster brothers, and sleeping less. Weekly coconut oil skin rubs helped, and he now has a normal Cocker cut. I was thrilled when I first heard Moe bark, mimicking his foster brother. It's a joy watching my Cockers teach him how to be a dog.

Shortly after Moe's one-year anniversary of being rescued, he was only taking two daily doses of medications, and his prednisone dose was just 6% from his highest dosage; of course, the long-term goal is to eliminate the prednisone completely. Moe has become an ambassador of RMCR, with his gorgeous, long, black, silky ears and the almost-perfect white stripe separating his eyes and flowing to the top of his head.

The children who donated their allowance to Moe are now ambassadors for RMCR, and they visit Moe often. Moe grabs the attention of all who meet him, and everyone loves him in return. He is a true representative of why rescues exist and why saving and rehabilitating Cockers is one of RMCR's top priorities.

*Audra J. Bowen*

# About Happy Tails Books™

Schnauzer   Chihuahua   **Golden Retriever**   **PUG**
DACHSHUND   German Shepherd   Collie   **Boxer**
*Labrador Retriever*   Husky   Beagle   ALL AMERICAN
Border Collie   Pit Bull Terrier   Shih Tzu   Miniature Pinscher
Chow Chow   *Australian Shepherd*   Rottweiler   Greyhound
Boston Terrier   Jack Russell   *Poodle*   Cocker Spaniel
Doberman Pinscher   Yorkie   **SHEEPDOG**
GREAT DANE   ST. BERNARD   Pointer   Blue Heeler

Happy Tails Books™ was created to support animal rescue efforts by showcasing the love and joy adopted dogs have to offer. With the help of animal rescue groups, stories are submitted by people who have adopted dogs, and then Happy Tails Books™ compiles them into breed-specific books. These books serve not only to entertain but also to educate readers about dog adoption and the characteristics of each specific type of dog. Happy Tails Books™ donates a significant portion of proceeds back to the rescue groups that help gather stories for the books.

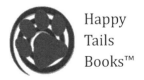

Happy Tails Books™

To submit a story or learn about other books Happy Tails Books™ publishes, please visit our website at http://happytailsbooks.com.

15731005R00083

Made in the USA
San Bernardino, CA
05 October 2014